My First 1000 SPANISH WORDS

Susan Martineau, Sam Hutchinson, Louise Millar, and Catherine Bruzzone

Illustrations by Stu McLellan
Spanish adviser: Diego Blasco Vázquez
Spanish advisor, Happy Fox edition: Rosi Perea

Sumario Contents

soo-MAH-ryoh

el bolígrafo
el boh-LEE-grah-foh
pen

el futbolito
el fuht-bohl-EE-toh
foosball table

**el niño/
la niña**
el NEE-nyoh/la NEE-nyah
child

el espacio de lectura
el ehs-PAH-syoh deh lehk-TOO-rah
reading corner

la pizarra blanca
lah pee-SAH-rrah BLAHN-kah
whiteboard

**los gemelos/
las gemelas**
lohs heh-MEH-lohs/heh-MEH-lahs
twins

el libro de texto
el LEE-broh deh TEHKS-toh
textbook

la puerta
lah PWEHR-tah
door

En la escuela
en la ehs-KWEH-lah
At school

el reloj
el rreh-LOHH
clock

el librero
el lee-BREH-roh
bookshelf

**el maestro/
la maestra**
el mah-EHS-troh/lah mah-EHS-trah
teacher

la tablet
lah TAHB-leht
tablet

la merienda
lah meh-RYEHN-dah
snack

las tijeras
lahs tee-HEH-rahs
scissors

el bolso escolar
el BOHL-soh ehs-coh-LAHR
book bag

la computadora
lah kohm-poo-tah-DOH-rah
computer

2

la silla
lah SEE-yah
chair

la clase
lah KLAH-seh
classroom

la regla
lah RREH-glah
ruler

los lápices de colores
lohs LAH-pee-sehs deh koh-LOH-rehs
colored pencils

el abecedario
el ah-beh-seh-DAH-ryoh
alphabet

el pegamento
el peh-gah-MEHN-toh
glue

el juego
el HWEH-goh
game

el cuadro
el KWAH-droh
painting

el pincel
el peen-SEHL
paintbrush

el papel
el pah-PEHL
paper

**el alumno/
la alumna**
el ah-LOOM-noh/lah ah-LOOM-nah
student

la goma de borrar
lah GOH-mah deh boh-RRAHR
eraser

la mochila
lah moh-CHEE-lah
backpack

las pinturas
lahs peen-TOO-rahs
paints

el pupitre
el poo-PEE-treh
desk

el póster
el POHS-tehr
poster

el director/la directora
el dee-rehk-TOHR/lah dee-rehk-TOHR-ah
principal

el lápiz
el LAH-pees
pencil

3

la cometa
lah koh-MEH-tah
kite

la carriola
lah kah-RRYOH-lah
stroller

la pluma
lah PLOO-mah
feather

El parque
el PAHR-keh
The park

el árbol
el AHR-bohl
tree

el puente
el PWEHN-teh
bridge

el renacuajo
el rreh-nah-KWAH-hoh
tadpole

el búho
el BOO-oh
owl

el minigolf
el mee-nee-GOHLF
miniature golf

el columpio
el koh-LOOM-pyoh
swing

el palo
el PAH-loh
stick

la resbaladilla
lah rrehs-bah-lah-DEE-yah
slide

el poni
el POH-nee
pony

el sube y baja
el SOO-beh ee BAH-hah
seesaw

el arenero
ah-rreh-NEHR-roh
sandbox

el bote de remo
el BOH-teh deh RREH-moh
rowboat

el ping pong
el PEENG-pohng
ping pong table

los patines
lohs pah-TEE-nehs
rollerblades

4

el banco
el BAHN-koh
bench

el arbusto
el ahr-BOOS-toh
bush

palos para trepar
PAH-lohs PAH-rah treh-PAHR
jungle gym

la cerca
lah SEHR-kah
fence

la rana
lah RRAH-nah
frog

**el amigo/
la amiga**
*lohs ah-MEE-gohs/
las ah-MEE-gahs*
friend

el niño
el NEE-nyoh
boy

**los amigos/
las amigas**
*el ah-MEE-goh/
lah ah-MEE-gah*
friends

la niña
la NEE-nyah
girl

el ganso
el GAHN-soh
goose

**el corredor/
la corredora**
*el koh-rreh-DOHR/
lah koh-rreh-DOHR-ah*
jogger

el guardaparques
el GWAHR-dah-PAHR-kehs
park ranger

el río
el RREE-oh
stream

el remo
el RREH-moh
oar

el parque infantil
el PAHR-keh een-fahn-TEEL
playground

la paloma
lah pah-LOH-mah
pigeon

la cuerda de saltar
lah KWEHR-dah deh sahl-TAHR
jump rope

el tronco
el TROHN-koh
log

el quiosco
el KYOHS-koh
gazebo

el chapoteadero
el chah-poh-teh-ah-DEH-rroh
kiddie pool

5

el perico
el peh-REE-koh
parrot

el tigre
el TEE-greh
tiger

En el zoológico
en el soh-oh-LOH-hee-koh
At the zoo

la cebra
lah SEH-brah
zebra

la lagartija
lah lah-gahr-TEE-hah
lizard

el mono
el MOH-noh
monkey

el refugio
el rreh-FOO-hyoh
shelter

la cuerda
lah KWEHR-dah
rope

el hipopótamo
el ee-poh-POH-tah-moh
hippopotamus

el oso polar
el OH-soh poh-LAHR
polar bear

la morsa
lah MOHR-sah
walrus

el reno
el RREH-noh
reindeer

el pingüino
el peen-GWEE-noh
penguin

la víbora
lah BEE-boh-rah
snake

el panda
el PAHN-dah
panda

la nutria
lah NOO-tryah
otter

el rinoceronte
el rree-noh-seh-ROHN-teh
rhinoceros

la suricata
lah suh-rih-KAH-tah
meerkat

el aviario
el ah-bee-AH-ryoh
aviary

el león
el lee-OHN
lion

el koala
el koh-AH-lah
koala

el canguro
el kahn-GOO-roh
kangaroo

los animales
lohs ah-nee-MAHL-ehs
animals

la jirafa
lah hee-RAH-fah
giraffe

el cactus
el KAHK-toos
cactus

el mapache
el mah-PAH-cheh
raccoon

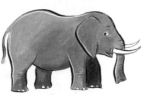

el elefante
el eh-leh-FAHN-teh
elephant

el camaleón
lah kah-mah-leh-OHN
chameleon

la madriguera
lah mah-dree-GEH-rah
burrow

el gorila
el goh-REE-lah
gorilla

el oso grizzly
el OH-soh GRIS-lee
grizzly bear

el cocodrilo
el koh-koh-DREE-loh
crocodile

el murciélago
el moor-see-EH-lah-goh
bat

el castor
el KAHS-tohr
beaver

el lobo
el LOH-boh
wolf

la jungla
lah HOON-glah
jungle

la jaula
lah HOW-lah
cage

7

el tractor
el trahk-TOHR
tractor

el remolque
rreh-MOHL-keh
trailer

La granja
lah GRAHN-hah

The farm

el campo
el KAHM-poh
field

la escoba
lah ehs-KOH-bah
broom

las botas de agua
lahs BOH-tahs deh AH-gwah
rain boots

el comedero
el koh-meh-DEH-roh
trough

el perro pastor
el PEH-rroh pahs-TOHR
sheepdog

el pastor
el pahs-TOHR
shepherd

el espantapájaros
el ehs-pahn-tah-PAH-hah-rohs
scarecrow

el heno
el EH-noh
hay

el corral
el koh-RRAHL
yard

la rata
lah RAH-tah
rat

el conejo
el koh-NEH-hoh
rabbit

el costal
el kohs-TAHL
sack

la moto
lah MOH-toh
all-terrain vehicle (ATV)

el cerdito
el sehr-DEE-toh
piglet

el cerdo
el SEHR-doh
pig

el panal
el pah-NAHL
beehive

el pato
el PAH-toh
duck

el patito
el pah-TEE-toh
duckling

el lodo
el LOH-doh
mud

el becerro
el beh-SEH-rroh
calf

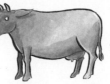
la vaca
lah BAH-kah
cow

la gallina
lah gah-YEE-nah
chicken

el pollito
el poh-YEE-toh
chick

el granero
el grah-NEHR-roh
barn

el cuervo
el KWEHR-boh
crow

el tejón
el teh-HOHN
badger

la granja
lah GRAHN-hah
farmhouse

el trigo
el TREE-goh
wheat

el huerto
el WEHR-toh
orchard

la cabra
lah KAH-brah
goat

el cabrito
el kah-BREE-toh
kid

el borrego
el boh-RREH-goh
lamb

la oveja
la oh-BEH-hah
sheep

el potro
el POH-troh
foal

el caballo
el kah-BAH-yoh
horse

la recolectora
lah rreh-coh-lehk-TOHR-ah
combine harvester

la vajilla sucia
lah bah-HEE-yah SOO-syah
dirty dishes

el cereal
el seh-reh-AHL
cereal

La cocina
lah koh-SEE-nah

The kitchen

la tetera
lah teh-TEH-rah
teapot

la tacita
lah tah-SEE-tah
sippy cup

la lavadora
lah lah-bah-DOH-rah
washing machine

el plato
el PLAH-toh
plate

el platillo
el plah-TEE-yoh
saucer

la tostada
lah tohs-TAH-dah
toast

los pañuelos desechables
lohs pah-NYWEH-lohs dehs-eh-CHAH-blehs
tissues

el cuchillo
el koo-CHEE-yoh
knife

el trapo de cocina
el TRAH-poh deh koh-SEE-nah
dish towel

la cuchara
lah koo-CHAR-rah
spoon

la mesa
lah MEH-sah
table

la olla
lah OH-yah
pot

el té
el TEH
tea

el fregadero
el freh-gah-DEHR-oh
sink

el taburete
el tah-boo-REH-teh
stool

el agua
el AH-gwah
water

el café
el kah-FEH
coffee

el babero
el bah-BEHR-roh
bib

la taza
lah TAH-sah
cup

la huevera
lah way-BAIR-ah
egg cup

la ventana
lah behn-TAH-nah
window

el tazón
el tah-SOHN
bowl

el desayuno
el deh-sah-YOO-noh
breakfast

el delantal
el deh-lahn-TAHL
apron

la estufa
el eh-STOO-fah
stove

el tenedor
el teh-neh-DOHR
fork

el refrigerador
el rreh-free-he-rah-DOHR
fridge

el vaso
el BAH-soh
glass

la silla para bebé
lah SEE-yah PAH-rah beh-BEH
highchair

la pasta
lah PAHS-tah
pasta

el jugo de naranja
el HOO-goh deh nah-RAHN-hah
orange juice

la leche
lah LEH-cheh
milk

la carta
lah KAHR-tah
letter

la mermelada
lah mehr-meh-LAH-dah
jam

el wok
el WOHK
wok

11

la casita del árbol
lah kah-SEE-tah dehl AHR-bohl
treehouse

la carretilla
lah kah-rreh-TEE-yah
wheelbarrow

El huerto
el WEHR-toh

The backyard

la flor
lah FLOHR
flower

la hoja
lah OH-hah
leaf

la lombriz
lah lohm-BREES
worm

la regadera de plantas
ah rreh-gah-DEH-rah deh PLAHN-tahs
watering can

el tinaco
el tee-NAH-koh
rain barrel

el caracol
el kah-rah-KOHL
snail

la madera
lah mah-DEH-rah
wood

el hacha
el AH-cha
axe

el rastrillo
el rrahs-TREE-yoh
rake

la araña
lah ah-RAH-nyah
spider

la pared
lah pah-REHD
wall

el cobertizo
el koh-behr-TEE-soh
shed

el serrucho
el seh-RROO-choh
saw

la espátula
el ehs-PAH-too-lah
trowel

el estanque
el ehs-TAHN-keh
pond

el camino
el kah-MEE-noh
path

el manzano
el mahn-SAH-noh
apple tree

el seto
el SEH-toh
hedge

el pasto
el PAHS-toh
lawn

la puerta
lah PWEHR-tah
gate

la canasta
lah kah-NAH-stah
basket

la rama
lah RAH-mah
branch

el garage
el gah-RAH-heh
garage

pila para hacer compost
PEE-lah PAH-rah ah-SEHR kohm-POHST
compost pile

la hierba
lah YEHR-bah
grass

el invernadero
el een-behr-nah-DEH-roh
greenhouse

el martillo
el mahr-TEE-yoh
hammer

el comedero de pájaros
el koh-meh-DEH-roh deh PAH-hah-rohs
bird feeder

la manguera
lah mahn-GEH-rah
hose

la escalera
lah ehs-kah-LEH-rah
ladder

el cortacésped
el kohr-tah-SEHS-pehd
lawnmower

el clavo
el KLAH-boh
nail

la caja de herramientas
lah KAH-hah deh eh-rrah-MYEHN-tahs
tool box

la maceta
lah mah-SEH-tah
flower pot

el huerto de verduras
el WEHR-toh deh behr-DOO-rahs
vegetable patch

el gatito
el gah-TEE-toh
kitten

El baño y el dormitorio

el BAH-nyoh ee el dohr-mee-TOH-ryoh

The bathroom and the bedroom

el despertador
el dehs-pehr-tah-DOHR
alarm clock

la ducha
lah DOO-chah
shower

la toalla
lah toh-AH-yah
towel

el lavabo
el lah-BAH-boh
sink

la pasta de dientes
lah PAHS-tah deh DYEHN-tehs
toothpaste

el cepillo de dientes
el seh-PEE-yoh deh DYEHN-tehs
toothbrush

el inodoro
el een-oh-DOH-roh
toilet

el papel higiénico
el pah-PEHL ee-HYEH-nee-koh
toilet paper

la tina
lah TEE-nah
bath

la esponja
lah ehs-POHN-hah
sponge

el jabón
el hah-BOHN
soap

el champú
el chahm-POO
shampoo

la sábana
lah sah-BAH-nah
sheet

la almohada
lah ahl-moh-HAH-dah
pillow

el celular
el seh-LOO-lahr
cell phone

el osito de peluche
el oh-SEE-toh deh peh-LOO-cheh
teddy bear

la cama
lah KAH-mah
bed

la mesita de noche
lah meh-SEE-tah deh NOH-cheh
bedside table

la cómoda
lah KOH-moh-dah
dresser

la cobija
lah koh-BEE-hah
blanket

el armario
el ahr-MAH-ryoh
wardrobe

la cuna
lah KOO-nah
crib

las cortinas
lahs kohr-TEE-nahs
curtains

la lámpara de escritorio
lah lahm-PAH-rah deh ehs-kree-TOH-ryoh
desk lamp

la colcha
lah KOHL-chah
comforter

el cepillo del cabello
el seh-PEE-yoh dehl kah-BEH-yoh
hairbrush

el baúl
el bah-OOL
chest

el hámster
el AHM-stehr
hamster

el espejo
el ehs-PEH-hoh
mirror

el tapete
el tah-PEH-teh
bath mat

el joyero
el hoh-YEH-roh
jewelry box

los audífonos
lohs ow-DEE-foh-nohs
headphones

la casa
lah KAH-sa
house

el peine
el PEY-neh
comb

En casa

en KAH-sah

At home

el departamento
el deh-pahr-tah-MEHN-toh
appartment

los muebles
lohs MWEH-blehs
furniture

el teléfono
el teh-LEH-foh-noh
telephone

la aspiradora
lah ahs-pee-rah-DOH-rah
vacuum cleaner

la televisión
lah teh-leh-bee-SYOHN
television

la madriguera del ratón
lah mah-dree-GEH-rah dehl rah-TOHN
mouse hole

las manchas
lahs MAHN-chahs
stains

las bocinas
lahs boh-SEE-nahs
speakers

el sofá
el soh-FAH
couch

la sala
lah SAH-lah
living room

la radio
lah RAH-dee-oh
radio

el tapete
el tah-PEH-teh
rug

el perro
el PEH-rroh
dog

la jarra de agua
lah HAH-rrah deh AH-gwah
pitcher of water

el reposapiés
el reh-poh-sah-pee-EHS
footstool

el cuadro
el KWAH-droh
picture

la botella
lah boh-TEH-yah
bottle

la servilleta
lah sehr-bee-YEH-tah
napkin

el techo
el TEH-choh
ceiling

el posavasos
el poh-sah-BAH-sohs
coaster

la alacena
lah ah-lah-SEH-nah
cabinet

el cojín
el koh-HEEN
cushion

el comedor
el koh-meh-DOHR
dining room

el cachorro
el kah-CHOHR-roh
puppy

el aparador
el ah-pah-rah-DOHR
sideboard/buffet

el DVD
el deh-beh-DEH
DVD

la planta
lah PLAHN-tah
plant

el sillón
el see-YOHN
armchair

el florero
el floh-REHR-oh
vase

el piso
el PEE-soh
floor

la llave
lah YAH-beh
key

el control remoto
el kohn-TROHL rreh-MOH-toh
remote control

el gato
el GAH-toh
cat

el ratón
el rah-TOHN
mouse

la comida
lah koh-MEE-dah
meal

la laptop
lah LAHP-tohp
laptop

la pantalla
lah pahn-TAH-yah
lampshade

la lámpara
lah LAHM-pah-rah
lamp

17

el faro
el FAH-roh
lighthouse

La playa y el fondo del mar

lah PLAH-yah ee el FOHN-doh dehl mahr

Beach and under the sea

la pala
lah PAH-lah
shovel

la gaviota
lah gah-BYOH-tah
seagull

la ballena
lah bah-YEH-nah
whale

la ola
lah OH-lah
wave

el traje de baño
el TRAH-heh deh BAH-nyoh
swimsuit

el chaleco salvavidas
el chah-LEH-koh sahl-bah-BEE-dahs
lifejacket

los lentes de sol
lohs LEHN-tehs deh sohl
sunglasses

el bloqueador
el bloh-keh-ah-DOHR
sunscreen

el castillo de arena
el kahs-TEE-yah deh ah-REH-nah
sandcastle

la concha
lah KOHN-chah
shell

el tiburón
el tee-boo-ROHN
shark

el alga marina
ehl AHL-gah mah-REE-nah
seaweed

la tabla de surf
lah TAH-blah deh suhrf
surfboard

el/la surfista
el/lah suhr-FEE-stah
surfer

 **el cangrejo**
el kahn-GREH-hoh
crab

 la cubeta
lah koo-BEH-tah
bucket

 la boya
lah BOH-yah
buoy

 **el barco de pesca**
el BAHR-koh deh PEHS-kah
fishing boat

 las papas fritas
lahs PAH-pahs FREE-tahs
french fries

 la silla de playa
lah SEE-yah deh PLAH-yah
deckchair

 **la sombrilla**
lah sohm-BREE-yah
beach umbrella

 **el acantilado**
el ah-kahn-tee-LAH-doh
cliff

 **la bucea-dora**
lah boo-seh-ah-DOHR-ah
scuba diver

 el coral
el koh-RAHL
coral

 la estrella de mar
la ehs-TREH-yah deh mahr
starfish

 **el delfín**
el dehl-FEEN
dolphin

 el pez
el PEHS
fish

 el algodón de azúcar
el ahl-goh-DOHN deh ah-SOO-kahr
cotton candy

 **la medusa**
lah meh-DOO-sah
jellyfish

 la arena
lah ah-REH-nah
sand

el pulpo
el POOL-poh
octopus

el naufragio
el now-FRAH-hyoh
shipwreck

la langosta
lah lahn-GOHS-tah
lobster

 la pelota de playa
lah peh-LOH-tah deh PLAH-yah
beach ball

el velero
el beh-LEH-roh
yacht

 **el salvavidas**
el sahl-bah-BEE-dahs
life preserver

 **la lancha**
lah LAHN-chah
dinghy

19

En el campo

en el KAHM-poh

In the countryside

el campamento
el kahm-pah-MEHN-toh
campsite

el bastón
el bah-STOHN
walking stick

las botas
lahs BOH-tahs
walking boots

el sendero
el sehn-DEHR-oh
trail

el viñedo
el bee-NYEH-doh
vineyard

la tienda de campaña
lah TYEHN-dah deh kahm-PAH-nah
tent

el río
el RREE-oh
river

la cascada
lah kahs-KAH-dah
waterfall

la ardilla
lah ahr-DEE-yah
squirrel

el picnic
el PEEK-neek
picnic

el cartel
el kahr-TEHL
signpost

el sándwich
el SAHND-weech
sandwich

el escarabajo
el ehs-kah-rah-BAH-hoh
beetle

los binoculares
lohs bee-noh-koo-LAH-rehs
binoculars

la roca
lah ROH-kah
rock

el remo
el REH-moh
paddle

la bicicleta de montaña
lah bee-see-KLEH-tah deh mohn-TAH-nyah
mountain bike

el pájaro
el PAH-hah-roh
bird

el oso pardo
el OH-soh PAHR-doh
brown bear

la mariposa
lah mah-ree-POH-sah
butterfly

las piedras
lahs PYEH-drahs
stones

la grulla
lah GROO-yah
crane

la canoa
lah kah-NOH-ah
canoe

la oruga
lah oh-ROO-gah
caterpillar

el cisne
el SEES-neh
swan

la cría del cisne
KREE-ah dehl SEES-neh
baby swan

el venado
el beh-NAH-doh
deer

el fuego
el FWEH-goh
fire

pescar
pehs-KAHR
fishing

la mosca
lah MOHS-kah
fly

el bosque
el BOHS-keh
forest

el zorro
el SOH-rroh
fox

la montaña
lah mohn-TAH-nyah
mountain

el mosquito
el mohs-KEE-toh
mosquito

el mapa
el MAH-pah
map

el lago
el LAH-goh
lake

las vacaciones
lahs bah-kah-SYOHN-ehs
vacation

la colina
lah koh-LEE-nah
hill

21

La tienda de libros y juguetes

lah TYEHN-dah deh LEE-brohs ee hoo-GEH-tehs

Book store and toy store

los bloques
lohs BLOH-kehs
blocks

el xilófono
el see-LOH-foh-noh
xylophone

la trompeta
lah trohm-PEH-tah
trumpet

el triciclo
el tree-SEE-kloh
tricycle

los juguetes
lohs hoo-GEH-tehs
toys

la caja registradora
lah CAH-hah rreh-hees-trah-DOHR-ah
cash register

el disfraz de superhéroe
el dees-FRAHS deh soo-pehr-eh-ROH-eh
superhero costume

los dados
lohs DAH-dohs
dice

el robot
el rroh-BOHT
robot

el libro de cuentos
el LEE-broh deh KWEHN-tohs
storybook

el avión armable
el ah-BYOHN ahr-MAH-bleh
model airplane

el rompecabezas
el rohm-peh-kah-BEH-sahs
jigsaw puzzle

el librero
el lee-BREH-roh
shelf

el caballo mecedor
el kah-BAH-yoh meh-seh-DOHR
rocking horse

el libro
el LEE-broh
book

los peluches
lohs peh-LOO-chehs
stuffed animals

los platillos
lohs plah-TEE-yohs
cymbals

el castillo
el kahs-TEE-yoh
castle

el tambor
el TAHM-bohr
drum

el diccionario
el deek-syoh-NAH-ryoh
dictionary

la casa de muñecas
lah KAH-sah deh moo-NYEH-kahs
doll house

la muñeca
lah moo-NYEH-kah
doll

el dominó
el doh-mee-NOH
dominoes

los zancos
lohs SAHN-kohs
stilts

el globo terráqueo
el GLOH-boh teh-RRAH-keh-oh
globe

la guitarra
lah gee-TAH-rrah
guitar

los títeres
lohs TEE-teh-rehs
puppets

el monedero
el moh-neh-DEH-roh
purse

la flauta
lah FLOW-tah
recorder

el trenecito de juguete
el treh-neh-SEE-toh deh hoo-GEH-teh
toy train

el juego de magia
el HWEH-goh deh MAH-hyah
magic set

el dinero
el dee-NEH-roh
money

la tienda
lah TYEHN-dah
store

los vehículos
lohs bee-EE-koo-lohs
vehicles

la camioneta
lah kah-myoh-NEH-tah
van

el túnel
el TOO-nehl
tunnel

el barco
el BAHR-koh
boat

el billete
el bee-YEH-teh
ticket

el ferry
FEH-rree
ferry

el puerto
el PWEHR-toh
port

el carguero
el kahr-GEH-roh
container ship

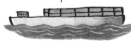
la maleta
lah mah-LEH-tah
suitcase

la señal
lah seh-NYAHL
signal

El transporte
el trahns-POHR-teh
Transportation

el aeropuerto
el ah-eh-roh-PWEHR-toh
airport

el barco
el BAHR-koh
ship

el asiento
el ah-SYEHN-toh
seat

el tren
el trehn
train

los rieles
lohs RYEHL-ehs
train tracks

la estación de tren
lah ehs-tah-SYOHN deh trehn
train station

el paso a nivel
el PAH-soh ah nee-BEHL
railroad crossing

24

el avión
el ah-BYOHN
airplane

la excavadora
lah ehks-kah-bah-DOH-rah
excavator

el volquete
el bohl-KEH-teh
dump truck

el ladrillo
el lah-DREE-yoh
brick

el bulldozer
el bool-doh-SEHR
bulldozer

el helicóptero
el eh-lee-KOHP-teh-roh
helicopter

el camión de mezcla
el kah-MYOHN deh MEHS-klah
cement mixer

el andamio
el ahn-DAH-myoh
scaffolding

la escalera mecánica
lah ehs-kah-LEH-rah meh-KAH-nee-kah
escalator

el autobús
el ow-toh-BOOS
bus

el camión de bomberos
el kah-MYOHN deh bohm-BEH-rohs
fire engine

el elevador
el ehl-eh-bah-DOHR
elevator

el andén
el ahn-DEHN
platform

la motocicleta
lah moh-toh-see-KLEH-tah
motorcycle

el coche de policía
el KOH-cheh deh poh-lee-SEE-ah
police car

el equipaje
el eh-kee-PAH-heh
luggage

el camión
el kah-MYOHN
semi/tractor trailer

la zona de construcción
lah SOH-nah deh kohns-trook-SYOHN
construction site

En la ciudad
en lah see-oo-DAHD

In the city

el cine
el SEE-neh
movie theater

la glorieta
lah gloh-RYEH-tah
roundabout

el cartero
lah kahr-TEH-roh
mail carrier

**la bolsa
del cartero**
lah BOHL-sah dehl kahr-TEH-roh
mailbag

el buzón
el boo-SOHN
mailbox

**la oficina
de correos**
*lah oh-fee-SEE-nah
deh koh-RREH-ohs*
post office

el semáforo
el seh-MAH-foh-roh
traffic light

la panadería
lah pah-nah-deh-REE-ah
bakery

el paso peatonal
el PAH-soh peh-ah-toh-NAHL
crosswalk

**la tienda
de mascotas**
lah TYEHN-dah deh mahs-KOH-tahs
pet store

la calle
lah KAH-yeh
road

el baño público
el BAHN-yoh POO-blee-koh
public restroom

el paraguas
el pah-RAH-gwahs
umbrella

el puesto
el PWEHS-toh
stall

el restaurante
el rrehs-tah-RAHN-teh
restaurant

el coche
el KOH-cheh
car

la fábrica
lah FAH-bree-kah
factory

la bicicleta
lah bee-see-KLEH-tah
bicycle

el bote de basura
el BOH-teh deh bah-SOO-rah
trash can

la acera
la ah-SEH-rah
sidewalk

la bandera
lah bahn-DEH-rah
flag

la carnicería
lah kahr-nee-seh-REE-ah
butcher shop

el café
el kah-FEH
café

la farmacia
lah fahr-MAH-syah
pharmacy

el banco
el BAHN-koh
bank

el hotel
el oh-TEHL
hotel

la biblioteca
lah bee-blyoh-TEH-kah
library

la gasolinera
lah gah-soh-lee-NEH-rah
gas station

la parada del autobús
lah pah-RAH-dah dehl ow-toh-BOOS
bus stop

la oficina
lah oh-fee-SEE-nah
office

el museo
el moo-SEH-oh
museum

la señal de tráfico
la seh-NYAHL deh TRAH-fee-koh
traffic sign

el mercado
el mehr-KAH-doh
farmers' market

27

la bruja
lah BROO-hah
witch

la tiara
lah tee-AH-rah
tiara

La fiesta
lah fee-EH-stah
The party

las salchichas
lahs sahl-CHEE-chahs
cocktail sausages

el globo
el GLOH-boh
balloon

el violín
el byoh-LEEN
violin

la serpentina
lah sehr-pehn-TEE-nah
streamer

la reina
lah REH-nah
queen

la princesa
lah preen-SEH-sah
princess

el príncipe
el PREEN-see-peh
prince

la sirena
lah see-REH-nah
mermaid

el pirata
el pee-RAH-tah
pirate

el sombrero de fiesta
el sohm-BREH-roh deh fee-EH-stah
party hat

el vestido de fiesta
el behs-TEE-doh deh fee-EH-stah
party dress

el matasuegras
el mah-tah-SWEH-grahs
party blower

el gigante
el hee-GAHN-teh
giant

la música
lah MOO-see-kah
music

los quequis
lohs KEH-kees
cupcakes

el collar de cuentas
el koh-YAHR deh KWEHN-tahs
beads

el helado
el eh-LAH-doh
ice cream

la pizza
lah PEE-sah
pizza

el regalo
el rreh-GAH-loh
present

el chocolate
el choh-koh-LAH-teh
chocolate

el hada
lah AH-dah
fairy

el refresco
el rreh-FREHS-koh
soda

la corona
lah koh-ROH-nah
crown

la vela
lah BEH-lah
candle

el caballero
el kah-bah-YEH-roh
knight

la capa
lah KAH-pah
cloak

las zapatillas de ballet
lahs sah-pah-TEE-yahs deh bah-LEHT
ballet slippers

el genio
el HEH-nyoh
genie

el rey
el REH
king

el dragón
el drah-GOHN
dragon

el jugo de fruta
el HOO-goh deh FROO-tah
fruit juice

la varita mágica
lah bah-REE-tah MAH-hee-kah
magic wand

la limonada
lah lee-moh-NAH-dah
lemonade

la paleta de caramelo
lah pah-LEH-tah deh kah-rah-MEH-loh
lollipop

la lámpara mágica
lah LAHM-pah-rah MAH-hee-kah
magic lamp

los vegetales
llohs beh-heh-TAHL-ehs
vegetables

El supermercado
el soo-pehr-mehr-KAH-doh
The supermarket

la manzana
lah mahn-SAH-nah
apple

el yogurt
el yoh-GOORT
yogurt

el carrito
el kah-RREE-toh
shopping cart

el tomate
el toh-MAH-teh
tomato

la fresa
lah FREHS-kah
strawberry

la bolsa de compras
lah BOHL-sah deh KOHM-prahs
shopping bag

la ensalada
lah ehs-kah-LAH-dah
salad

el arroz
el ah-RROHS
rice

la papa
lah PAH-pah
potato

la piña
lah PEE-nyah
pineapple

la pera
lah PEH-rah
pear

el durazno
el doo-RAHS-noh
peach

la naranja
lah nah-RAHN-hah
orange

la cebolla
lah seh-BOH-yah
onion

el mango
el MAHN-go
mango

el limón
el lee-MOHN
lemon

la lechuga
lah leh-CHUH-gah
lettuce

la berenjena
lah beh-rehn-HEH-nah
eggplant

el plátano
el PLAH-tah-noh
banana

las galletas
lahs gah-YEH-tahs
cookies

el pan
el PAHN
bread

la mantequilla
lah mahn-teh-KEE-yah
butter

la col
lah KOHL
cabbage

el pastel
el pahs-TEHL
cake

la zanahoria
lah sah-nah-OH-ryah
carrot

el apio
el AH-pyoh
celery

el queso
el KEH-soh
cheese

la cereza
lah seh-REH-sah
cherry

el pollo
el POH-yoh
chicken

el maíz
el mah-EES
corn

el calabacín
el kah-lah-bah-SEEN
zucchini

el pepino
el peh-PEE-noh
cucumber

el kiwi
el KEE-wee
kiwi

el jamón
el hah-MOHN
ham

las uvas
lahs OO-bahs
grapes

la fruta
lah FROO-tah
fruit

la comida
lah koh-MEE-dah
food

el pescado
el pehs-KAH-doh
fish

los huevos
lohs WEH-bohs
egg

los deportes
lohs deh-POHR-tehs
sport

En el centro deportivo
en el SEHN-troh deh-pohr-TEE-boh
At the rec center

la carrera
lah kah-RREH-rah
race

el yoga
el YOH-gah
yoga

el silbato
el seel-BAH-toh
whistle

la silla de ruedas
lah SEE-yah deh RRWEH-dah
wheelchair

la cancha de tenis
lah KAHN-chah deh TEH-nees
tennis court

el tenis
el TEH-nees
tennis

el equipo
el eh-KEE-poh
team

la línea de salida
lah LEE-neh-ah deh sah-LEE-dah
starting block

el equipo de deporte
el eh-KEE-poh deh deh-POHR-teh
sports gear

la maleta deportiva
lah mah-LEH-tah deh-pohr-TEE-bah
sports bag

la alberca
lah ahl-BEHR-kah
swimming pool

nadar
nah-DAHR
swimming

los esquís
lohs ehs-KEES
skis

esquiar
ehs-KYAHR
skiing

la pluma
lah PLOO-mah
shuttlecock

los aeróbicos
lohs ah-eh-ROH-bee-kohs
aerobics

el bádminton
BAHD-meen-ton
badminton

el atletismo
el aht-let-TEES-moh
athletics

el baloncesto
el bah-lohn-SEHS-toh
basketball

el vestidor
el behs-tee-DOHR
locker room

el partido de fútbol
el pahr-TEE-doh deh FOOT-bohl
soccer game

el trampolín
el trahm-poh-LEEN
diving board

el balón de fútbol
el bah-LOHN deh FOOT-bohl
soccer ball

la raqueta
lah rrah-KEH-tah
racket

el entrenador
el ehn-treh-nah-DOHR
coach

la pelota
lah peh-LOH-tah
ball

las gafas de buceo
lahs GAH-fahs deh boo-SEH-oh
goggles

la gimnasia
lah heem-NAH-syah
gymnastics

el salto de longitud
el SAHL-toh deh lohn-hee-TOOD
long jump

el marcador
el mahr-kah-DOHR
scoreboard

el sauna
el SOW-nah
sauna

el árbitro
el AHR-bee-troh
referee

el portero
el pohr-TEH-roh
goalie

el salto de altura
el SAHL-toh deh ahl-TOO-rah
high jump

Las palabras de acción

lahs pah-LAH-brahs deh ahk-SYOHN

Action words

estar parado
ehs-TAHR pah-RAH-doh
standing

andar
ahn-DAHR
walking

ver la tele
behr lah TEH-leh
watching TV

hablar
ah-BLAHR
talking

cocinar
koh-see-NAHR
cooking

estar sentado
ehs-TAHR sehn-TAH-doh
sitting

lavarse los dientes
lah-BAHR-seh lohs DYEHN-tehs
brushing your teeth

cargar
karh-GAHR
carrying

empujar
ehm-poo-HAHR
pushing

jalar
hah-LAHR
pulling

señalar
seh-nyah-LAHR
pointing

jugar
hoo-GAHR
playing

pintar
peen-TAHR
painting

saltar
sahl-TAHR
jumping

leer
leh-EHR
reading

cantar
kahn-TAHR
singing

dibujar
dee-boo-HAHR
drawing

escribir
ehs-kree-BEER
writing

gatear
gah-teh-AHR
crawling

andar en bicicleta
ahn-DAHR en bee-see-KLEH-tah
riding a bike

bailar
bay-LAHR
dancing

hacer voltereta lateral
ah-SEHR bohl-teh-REH-tah lah-tehr-AHL
doing a cartwheel

pararse de cabeza
pah-RAHR-seh deh kah-BEH-sah
doing a headstand

dar marometas
dahr mah-roh-MEH-tahs
doing somersaults

escalar
ehs-kah-LAHR
climbing

beber
beh-BEHR
drinking

comer
koh-MEHR
eating

besar
beh-SAHR
kissing

abrazar
ah-brah-SAHR
hugging

lavarse
lah-BAHR-seh
washing up

correr
kor-RREHR
running

acostarse
ah-kohs-TAHR-seh
going to sleep

levantarse
leh-bahn-TAHR-seh
getting up

Tu cuerpo

too KWEHR-poh

Your body

la cabeza
lah kah-BEH-sah
head

la oreja
lah oh-REH-hah
ear

la mejilla
lah meh-HEE-yah
cheek

el labio
el LAH-byoh
lip

la boca
lah BOH-kah
mouth

los dientes
lohs DYEHN-tehs
teeth

la barbilla
lah bahr-BEE-yah
chin

el brazo
el BRAH-soh
arm

la mano
lah MAH-noh
hand

las uñas
lahs OO-nahs
nails

el pecho
el PEH-choh
chest

el tobillo
el toh-BEE-yoh
ankle

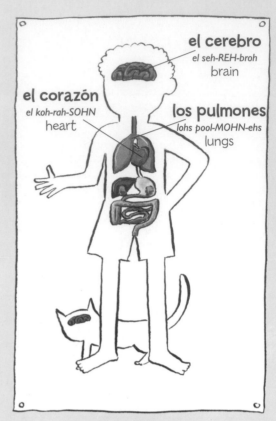

el cerebro
el seh-REH-broh
brain

el corazón
el koh-rah-SOHN
heart

los pulmones
lohs pool-MOHN-ehs
lungs

la espalda
lah ehs-PAHL-dah
back

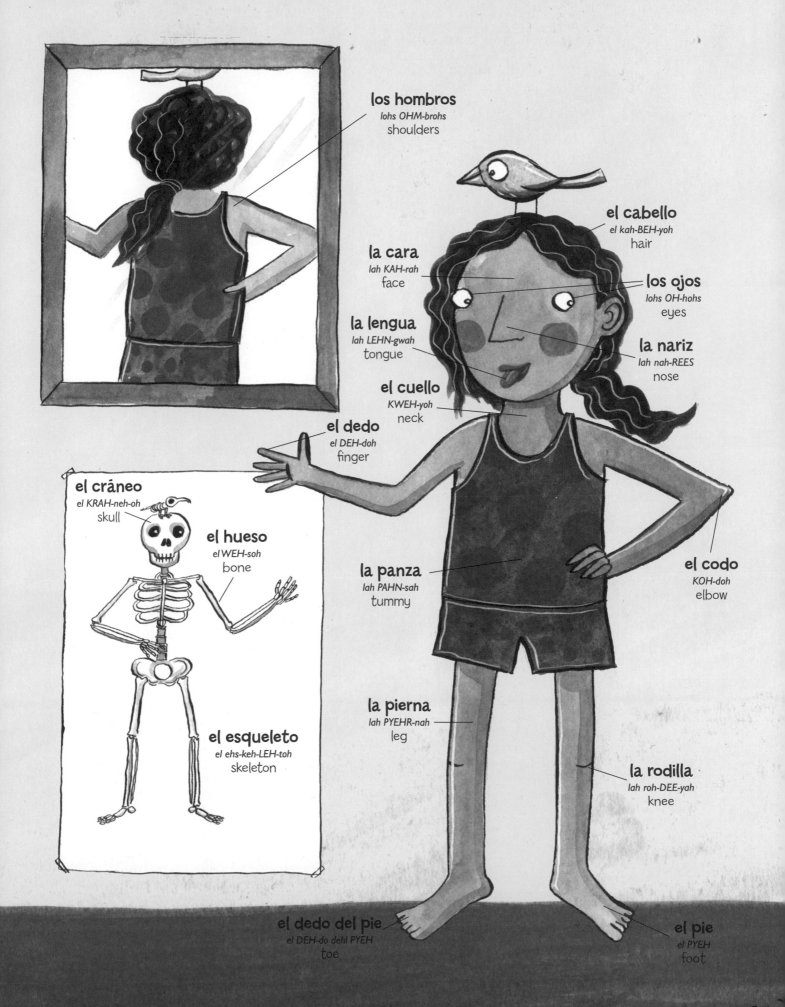

los hombros
lohs OHM-brohs
shoulders

el cabello
el kah-BEH-yoh
hair

la cara
lah KAH-rah
face

los ojos
lohs OH-hohs
eyes

la lengua
lah LEHN-gwah
tongue

la nariz
lah nah-REES
nose

el cuello
KWEH-yoh
neck

el dedo
el DEH-doh
finger

el cráneo
el KRAH-neh-oh
skull

el hueso
el WEH-soh
bone

la panza
lah PAHN-sah
tummy

el codo
KOH-doh
elbow

el esqueleto
el ehs-keh-LEH-toh
skeleton

la pierna
lah PYEHR-nah
leg

la rodilla
lah roh-DEE-yah
knee

el dedo del pie
el DEH-do dehl PYEH
toe

el pie
el PYEH
foot

Los colores y las formas

lohs koh-LOH-rehs ee lahs FOHR-mahs

Colors and shapes

el caballete
el kah-bah-YEH-teh
easel

la escultura
lah ehs-kool-TOO-rah
sculpture

el triángulo
el tree-AHN-goo-loh
triangle

el marco
el MAHR-koh
frame

el cubo
el KOO-boh
cube

el círculo
el SEER-koo-loh
circle

la media luna
lah MEH-dyah LOO-nah
crescent

el cuadrado
el kwah-DRAH-doh
square

el arco iris
el AHR-koh EE-rees
rainbow

la paleta
lah pah-LEH-tah
palette

el rectángulo
rrehk-TAHN-goo-loh
rectangle

la esfera
lah ehs-FEH-rah
sphere

el cilindro
el see-LEEN-droh
cylinder

la pirámide
lah pee-RAH-mee-deh
pyramid

el hexágono
el ehk-SAH-goh-noh
hexagon

ovalado/ovalada
oh-bah-LAH-doh/dah
oval

blanco/blanca
BLAHN-koh/ BLAHN-kah
white

negro/negra
NEH-groh/NEH-grah
black

azul
ah-SOOL
blue

amarillo/amarilla
ah-mah-REE-yoh/ ah-mah-REE-yah
yellow

café
kah-FEH
brown

violeta
byoh-LEH-tah
violet

el/la artista
el/lah ahr-TEES-tah
artist

turquesa
toor-KEH-sah
turquoise

morado/morada
moh-RAH-doh/ moh-RAH-dah
purple

rosa
ROH-sah
pink

rojo/roja
ROH-hoh/ ROH-hah
red

dorado
doh-RAH-doh
gold

plateado
play-teh-AH-doh
silver

verde
BEHR-deh
green

la galería de arte
lah gah-leh-REE-ah deh AHR-teh
art gallery

transparente
trahns-pah-REHN-teh
transparent

pálido/pálida
PAH-lee-doh/dah
pale

naranja
nah-RAHN-hah
orange

multicolor
mool-tee-koh-LOHR
multicolored

gris
GREES
gray

39

El árbol genealógico
el AHR-bohl heh-neh-ah-LOH-hee-koh
Family tree

los abuelos
lohs ah-BWEH-lohs
grandparents

el tío abuelo
el TEE-oh ah-BWEH-loh
great-uncle

el abuelo
el ah-BWEH-loh
grandfather

la abuela
lah ah-BWEH-lah
grandmother

la tía
lah TEE-ah
aunt

el tío
el TEE-oh
uncle

los primos/las primas
lohs PREE-mohs/lahs PREE-mahs
cousins

la sobrina
lah soh-BRREE-nah
niece

el sobrino
el soh-BRREE-noh
nephew

los bisabuelos
lohs bee-sah-BWEH-lohs
great-grandparents

la tía abuela
lah TEE-ah ah-BWEH-lah
great-aunt

las gemelas
lah heh-MEH-lahs
twins

los padres
lohs PAH-drehs
parents

mamá
mah-MAH
mom

la madre
lah MAH-dreh
mother

papá
pah-PAH
dad

el padre
el PAH-dreh
father

Mi familia
mee fah-MEE-lyah
My family

la hermana
lah ehr-MAH-nah
sister

el hermano
el ehr-MAH-noh
brother

el hijo
el EE-hoh
son

la hija
la EE-hah
daughter

el bebé
el beh-BEH
baby

los trillizos
lohs tree-YEE-sohs
triplets

el hospital
el ohs-pee-TAHL
hospital

En el hospital
en el ohs-pee-TAHL
In the hospital

la ambulancia
lah ahm-boo-LAHN-syah
ambulance

el cirujano
see-roo-HAH-noh
surgeon

los visitantes
lohs bee-see-TAHN-tehs
visitors

dolor de panza
doh-LOHR deh PAHN-sah
tummy ache

el tubo
el TOO-boh
tube

el quirófano
el kee-ROH-fah-noh
operating room

el estetoscopio
ehs-teh-tohs-KOH-pyoh
stethoscope

las pastillas
lahs pahs-TEE-yah
pills

los puntos
lohs POON-tohs
stitches

la sala de espera
lah SAH-lah deh ehs-PEH-rah
waiting room

dolor de cabeza
doh-LOHR de kah-BEH-sah
headache

el accidente
el ahk-see-DEHN-teh
accident

la venda
lah BEHN-dah
bandage

el buscapersonas
el BOOS-kah-pehr-SOH-nahs
pager

la gráfica
lah GRAH-fee-kah
chart

los instrumentos
lohs eens-troo-MEHN-tohs
instruments

el pasillo
el pah-SEE-yoh
hallway

el doctor/ la doctora
el dohk-TOHR/ lah dohk-TOHR-ah
doctor

el termómetro
el tehr-MOH-meh-toh
thermometer

la máquina de rayos X
lah MAH-kee-nah deh RRAH-yohs EHK-ees
x-ray machine

la inyección
lah een-yehk-SYOHN
injection

las muletas
lahs moo-LEH-tahs
crutches

la medicina
lah meh-dee-SEE-nah
medicine

la cafetería
lah kah-feh-teh-REE-ah
cafeteria

el cabestrillo
kah-behs-TREE-yoh
sling

la curita
lah koo-REE-tah
bandage

la operación
lah oh-peh-rah-SYOHN
operation

dolor de muelas
doh-LOHR deh MWEH-lahs
toothache

la radiografía
lah rrah-dyoh-grah-FEE-ah
x-ray

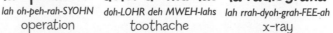
el enfermero/ la enfermera
el ehn-fehr-MEH-roh/ lah ehn-fehr-MEH-rah
nurse

43

Los oficios
lohs oh-FEE-syohs
Jobs

el mago
el MAH-goh
magician

el científico
el syehn-TEE-fee-koh
scientist

There is a different word for many of these jobs depending on whether you are a boy or a girl. They are all in the word list at the back of the book. On this page, you will find the version that goes with the picture.

la guarda del zoológico
lah GWAHR-dah dehl soh-oh-LOH-hee-koh
zookeeper

el vendedor
el behn-deh-DOHR
sales associate

la bailarina
lah bay-lah-REE-nah
dancer

el cobrador
el koh-brah-DOHR
ticket collector

el taxista
el tahk-SEES-tah
taxi driver

la secretaria
lah seh-kreh-TAH-ryah
secretary

la veterinaria
lah beh-teh-ree-NAH-ryah
vet

el basurero
bah-soo-REH-roh
sanitation worker

el cocinero
el koh-see-NEH-roh
chef

la estrella del pop
lah ehs-TREH-yah dehl pohp
singer

la policía
lah poh-lee-SEE-ah
police officer

la plomera
lah ploh-MEH-rah
plumber

el panadero
el pah-nah-DEH-roh
baker

el obrero
el oh-BREH-roh
construction worker

el chofer de autobús
el choh-FEHR deh ow-toh-BOOS
bus driver

el conductor
el kohn-dook-TOHR
conductor

la dentista
lah dehn-TEES-tah
dentist

el electricista
el eh-lehk-tree-SEES-tah
electrician

el carnicero
el kahr-NEH-roh
butcher

el granjero
el grahn-HEH-roh
farmer

el bombero
el bohm-BEH-roh
firefighter

la aeromoza
ah-eh-roh-MOH-sah
flight attendant

el futbolista
el foot-boh-LEES-tah
soccer player

el jardinero
el hahr-dee-NEHR-oh
gardener

el piloto
el pee-LOH-toh
pilot

la camionera
la kah-myoh-NEH-rah
truck driver

el salvavidas
el sahl-bah-BEE-dahs
lifeguard

el abogado
al ah-boh-GAH-doh
lawyer

la estilista
lah ehs-tee-LEES-tah
hairdresser

Los números

lohs NOO-meh-rohs

¿Cuántos hay? ¿Puedes descubrirlo? How many . . . can you find?

20 veinte
BEYN-teh
twenty

19 diecinueve
dyeh-see-NWEH-beh
nineteen

18 dieciocho
dyeh-see-OH-choh
eighteen

17 diecisiete
dyeh-see-SYEH-teh
seventeen

16 dieciséis
dyeh-see-SEYS
sixteen

15 quince
KEEN-seh
fifteen

14 catorce
kah-TOHR-seh
fourteen

13 trece
TREH-seh
thirteen

46

1 **uno/una**
OO-noh/OO-nah
one

2 **dos**
DOHS
two

3 **tres**
TREHS
three

4 **cuatro**
KWAH-tro
four

5 **cinco**
SEEN-koh
five

6 **seis**
SEYS
six

7 **siete**
SYEH-teh
seven

8 **ocho**
OH-choh
eight

9 **nueve**
NWEH-beh
nine

10 **diez**
DYEHS
ten

11 **once**
OHN-seh
eleven

12 **doce**
DOH-seh
twelve

12 **doce**
DOH-seh
twelve

11 **once**
OHN-seh
eleven

10 **diez**
DYEHS
ten

9 **nueve**
NWEH-beh
nine

47

Los opuestos

lohs oh-PWEHS-tohs

Opposites

lento/lenta
LEHN-toh/ LEHN-tah
slow

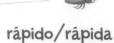

rápido/rápida
RAH-pee-doh/ RAH-pee-dah
fast

malo/mala
MAH-loh/lah
bad

bueno/buena
BWEH-noh/nah
good

desordenado/ desordenada
dehs-ohr-deh-NAH-doh/ dehs-ohr-deh-NAH-dah
messy

ordenado/ordenada
ohr-deh-NAH-doh/ ohr-deh-NAH-dah
neat

mojado/mojada
moh-HAH-doh/dah
wet

seco/seca
SEH-koh/kah
dry

ruidoso/ruidosa
rrwee-DOH-soh/sah
noisy

silencioso/silenciosa
see-lehn-SYOH-soh/sah
quiet

triste
TREES-teh
sad

feliz
feh-LEES
happy

largo/larga
LAHR-goh/gah
long

corto/ corta
KOHR-toh/tah
short

enfermo/ enferma
ehn-FEHR-moh/mah
sick

sano/ sana
SAH-noh/nah
healthy

48

enojado/ enojada
eh-noh-HAH-doh/dah
angry

tranquila/ tranquilo
trahn-KEE-loh/lah
calm

hermoso/hermosa
ehr-MOH-soh/sah
beautiful

feo/fea
FEH-oh/ah
ugly

grande
GRAHN-deh
big

pequeño/ pequeña
peh-KEH-nyoh/nyah
small

sucio/sucia
SOO-syoh/syah
dirty

limpio/limpia
LEEM-pyoh/pyah
clean

primero/primera
pree-MEH-roh/rah
first

último/última
OOL-tee-moh/mah
last

viejo/vieja
BYEH-hoh/ BYEH-hah
old

joven
HOH-behn
young

ligero/ligera
lee-HEH-roh/rah
light

diferente
dee-feh-REHN-teh
different

igual
ee-GWAHL
same

frío/fría
FREE-oh/ah
cold

caliente
kah-LYEHN-teh
hot

vacío/vacía
bah-SEE-oh/ah
empty

lleno/llena
YEH-noh/nah
full

pesado/pesada
peh-SAH-doh/dah
heavy

el astronauta
el ahs-troh-NOW-tah
astronaut

Espacio, tiempo y estaciones
ehs-PAH-syoh, TYEHM-poh ee ehs-tah-SYOHN-ehs
Space, weather, and seasons

el extraterrestre
ehks-trah-teh-RREHS-treh
alien

el invierno
el een-BYEHR-noh
winter

el viento
el BYEHN-toh
wind

la tormenta
lah tohr-MEHN-tah
storm

el tornado
el tohr-NAH-doh
tornado

el sol
el SOHL
sun

la estrella
lah ehs-TREH-yah
star

el verano
el beh-rah-noh
summer

el océano
el oh-SEH-ah-noh
ocean

el transbordador espacial
el trahns-bohr-dah-DOHR ehs-pah-SYAHL
space shuttle

el muñeco de nieve
el moo-NYEH-koh deh NYEH-beh
snowman

la nieve
lah NYEH-beh
snow

el cielo
el SYEH-loh
sky

el asteroide
el ahs-tehr-roh-EE-deh
asteroid

el OVNI
el OHB-nee
UFO

el continente
el kohn-tee-NEHN-teh
continent

la nube
lah NOO-beh
cloud

el cometa
el koh-MEH-tah
comet

el otoño
el oh-TOH-nyoh
fall

la Tierra
lah TYEH-rrah
Earth

la neblina
neh-BLEE-nah
fog

la galaxia
lah gah-LAHK-syah
galaxy

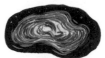

el granizo
el grah-NEE-soh
hail

el hielo
YEH-loh
ice

el relámpago
el rreh-LAHM-pah-goh
lightning

la luna
lah LOO-nah
moon

el satélite
el sah-TEH-lee-teh
satellite

el cohete
koh-EH-teh
rocket

la lluvia
lah YOO-byah
rain

la órbita
lah OHR-bee-tah
orbit

los planetas
lohs plah-NEH-tahs
planets

la primavera
lah pree-mah-BEH-rah
spring

51

la bolsa
lah BOHL-sah
purse

el reloj
el rreh-LOH
watch

La ropa
lah ROH-pah
Clothes

la pulsera
lah pool-SEH-rah
bracelet

la camisa
lah kah-MEE-sah
shirt

el pantalón
el pahn-tah-LOHN
pants

las medias
lahs MEH-dyahs
tights

la camiseta
lah kah-mee-SEH-tah
T-shirt

el pijama
el pee-HAH-mah
pajamas

las pantuflas
lahs pahn-TOO-flahs
slippers

los pantalones cortos
lohs pahn-tah-LOH-nehs KOHR-tohs
shorts

el cinturón
el seen-too-ROHN
belt

la bufanda
lah boo-FAHN-dah
scarf

los calcetines
lohs kahl-seh-TEEN-ehs
socks

el chaleco
el chah-LEH-koh
vest

las sandalias
lahs sahn-DAH-lyahs
sandals

el anillo
el ah-NEE-yoh
ring

los zapatos
lohs sah-PAH-tohs
shoes

el poncho
el POHN-choh
poncho

las botas
lahs BOH-tahs
boots

la falda
lah FAHL-da
skirt

la gorra
lah GOH-rrah
cap

el suéter abierto
el SWEH-tehr ah-BYEHR-toh
cardigan

el bolso
el BOHL-soh
bag

el vestido
el behs-TEE-doh
dress

las botas de fútbol
lahs BOH-tahs deh FOOT-bohl
cleats

los lentes
lohs LEHN-tehs
glasses

los guantes
lohs GWAHN-tehs
gloves

el abrigo
el ah-BREE-goh
coat

la chamarra
lah cha-MAH-rrah
jacket

el sombrero
sohm-BREH-roh
hat

el suéter
SWEH-tehr
sweater

el maquillaje
el mah-kee-YAH-heh
make-up

el bolsillo
el bohl-SEE-yoh
pocket

los calzones
lohs kahl-SOHN-ehs
underwear

el vestido de noche
el behs-TEE-doh deh NOH-cheh
nightgown

el collar
el koh-YAHRr
necklace

el esmalte de uñas
el ehs-MAHL-teh deh OO-nyahs
nail polish

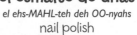

Palabras adicionales

pah-LAH-brahs ah-dee-syohn-AHL-ehs

Additional words

Here are some words that you will find useful as you practice Spanish at home.
They did not make it into the illustrated scenes in the book so they are gathered here for reference.
These words also appear in the word lists at the back of the book.

izquierda/izquierdo	derecho/derecha	delante de	Sra.	Sr.
ees-KYEHR-dah/ees-KYEHR-doh	deh-REH-choh/deh-REH-chah	deh-LAHN-teh deh	seh-NYOH-rah	seh-NYOHR
left	right	in front of	Mrs.	Mr.

mí	tú	ella	ella	él	él
MEE	TOO	EH-yah	EH-yah	EL	EL
me	you	she	her	he	him

enero	febrero	marzo	abril	mayo	junio
eh-NEH-roh	feh-BREH-roh	MAHR-soh	ah-BREEL	MAH-yoh	HOO-nyoh
January	February	March	April	May	June

julio	agosto	septiembre	octubre	noviembre	diciembre
HOO-lyoh	ah-GOHS-toh	sehp-TYEHM-breh	ohk-TOO-breh	noh-BYEHM-breh	dee-SYEHM-breh
July	August	September	October	November	December

lunes	martes	miércoles	jueves	viernes	sábado
LOO-nehs	MAHR-tehs	MYEHR-koh-lehs	HWEH-behs	BYEHR-nehs	SAH-bah-doh
Monday	Tuesday	Wednesday	Thursday	Friday	Saturday

domingo	hoy	ayer	mañana	la tarde	noche
doh-MEEN-goh	OY	ah-YEHR	mah-NYAH-nah	lah TAHR-deh	NOH-cheh
Sunday	today	yesterday	morning	afternoon	night

los días	los meses	el año	el cumpleaños	cien	mil
loh DEE-ahs	lohs MEHS-ehs	el AH-nyoh	koom-pleh-AH-nyohs	SYEHN	MEEL
days	months	year	birthday	hundred	thousand

brillante	vívido/vívida	oscuro	la competencia	el viaje	la altura
bree-YAHN-teh	BEE-bee-doh/BEE-bee-dah	ohs-KOO-roh	lah kohm-peh-TEHN-syah	el bee-AH-heh	lah ahl-TOO-rah
bright	vivid	dark	competition	travel	height

en/sobre	detrás	bajo	un abrazo	un beso	el peso
ehn/SOH-breh	deh-TRAHS	BAH-hoh	oon ah-BRAH-soh	oon BEH-soh	el PEH-soh
on	behind	under	hug	kiss	weight

el nombre
el NOHM-breh
name

Brief pronunciation notes

Throughout this book, pronunciation guides are included with each word. Here are some general rules to help you get started.

The vowel sounds are approximated this way in the pronunciation guides:
ah is like the short *a* in father
eh is like the short *e* in pet
ee is like the long *ee* sound in cheese
oh is like the long *o* in orange
oo is like the *oo* sound in food

When you see the *rr*, it means to roll or trill the *r* sound in that word.
The *d* in the pronunciation is often said more softly, and it can sound more similar to *th* when it is between two vowels.

Lista de palabras Word list

Spanish/español – English/inglés

el abecedario alphabet
la abogada (f) lawyer
el abogado (m) lawyer
abrazar hugging
abrazo hug
el abrigo coat
abril April
la abuela grandmother
el abuelo grandfather
los abuelos grandparents
el acantilado cliff
el accidente accident
la acera sidewalk
acostarse going to sleep
los aeróbicos aerobics
la aeromoza (f) flight attendant
el aeromozo (m) flight attendant
el aeropuerto airport
agosto August
el agua water
la alacena cabinet
la alberca swimming pool
el alga marina seaweed
el algodón de azúcar cotton candy
la almohada pillow
la altura height
la alumna (f) student
el alumno (m) student
amarillo yellow
la ambulancia ambulance
la amiga (f) friend
el amigo (m) friend
las amigas (f) friends
los amigos (m) friends
el andamio scaffolding
andar walking
andar en bicicleta riding a bike
el andén platform
el anillo ring
los animales animals
el año year
el aparador sideboard/buffet
el apio celery
la araña spider
el árbitro referee
el árbol tree
el árbol genealógico family tree
el arbusto bush
el arco iris rainbow
la ardilla squirrel

la arena sand
el arenero sandbox
el arroz rice
el armario wardrobe
el/la artista (m/f) artist
el asiento seat
la aspiradora vacuum cleaner
el asteroide asteroid
el astronauta astronaut
el atletismo athletics
los audífonos headphones
el autobús bus
el aviario aviary
el avión airplane
el avión armable model airplane
ayer yesterday
azul blue
el babero bib
el bádminton badminton
bailar dancing
el bailarín (m) dancer
la bailarina (f) dancer
bajo under
la ballena whale
el balón de fútbol soccer ball
el baloncesto basketball
el banco bank
el banco bench
la bandera flag
el baño bathroom
el baño público public restroom
la barbilla chin
el barco boat
el barco ship
el barco de pesca fishing boat
el bastón walking stick
la basurera (f) sanitation worker
el basurero (m) sanitation worker
el baúl chest
el bebé baby
beber drinking
el becerro calf
la berenjena eggplant
besar kissing
beso kiss
la biblioteca library
la bicicleta bicycle
la bicicleta de montaña mountain bike
el billete ticket

los binoculares binoculars
los bisabuelos great-grandparents
blanco/blanca white
el bloqueador sunscreen
los bloques blocks
la boca mouth
las bocinas speakers
el bolígrafo pen
la bolsa purse
la bolsa decompras shopping bag
la bolsa del cartero mailbag
el bolsillo pocket
el bolso bag
el bolso escolar book bag
la bombera (f) firefighter
el bombero (m) firefighter
el borrego lamb
el bosque forest
las botas boots
las botas walking boots
las botas de agua rain boots
las botas de fútbol cleats
el bote de basura trash can
el bote de remo rowboat
la botella bottle
la boya buoy
el brazo arm
brillante bright
la bruja witch
el buceador scuba diver
bueno/buena good
la bufanda scarf
el búho owl
el bulldozer bulldozer
el buscapersonas pager
el buzón mailbox
el caballero knight
el caballete easel
el caballo horse
el caballo mecedor rocking horse
el cabello hair
el cabestrillo sling
la cabeza head
la cabra goat
el cabrito kid (baby goat)
el cachorro puppy
el cactus cactus
café brown

el café coffee
el café café
la cafetería cafeteria
la caja de herramientas toolbox
la caja registradora cash register
el calabacín zucchini
los calcetines socks
caliente hot
la calle street/road
los calzones underwear
la cama bed
el camaleón chameleon
el camastro deckchair
el camino path
el camión semi/tractor trailer
el camión de bomberos fire engine
el camión de mezcla cement mixer
la camionera (f) truck driver
el camionero (m) truck driver
la camioneta van
la camisa shirt
la camiseta T-shirt
el campamento campsite
el campo field
el campo countryside
la canasta basket
la cancha de tenis tennis court
el cangrejo crab
el canguro kangaroo
la canoa canoe
cantar singing
la capa cloak
la cara face
el caracol snail
cargar carrying
el carguero container ship
la carnicera (f) butcher
la carnicería butcher shop
el carnicero (m) butcher
la carrera race
la carretilla wheelbarrow
la carriola stroller
el carrito shopping cart
la carta letter
el cartel signpost
el cartero mail carrier
la casa house
la casa home

Spanish/español - English/inglés

la casa de muñecas doll house
la cascada waterfall
la casita del árbol treehouse
el castillo castle
el castillo de arena sandcastle
el castor beaver
catorce fourteen
la cebolla onion
la cebra zebra
el celular cell phone
el centro deportivo rec center
el cepillo del cabello hairbrush
el cepillo de dientes
  toothbrush
la cerca fence
el cerdito piglet
el cerdo pig
el cereal cereal
el cerebro brain
la cereza cherry
el chaleco vest
el chaleco salvavidas life jacket
la chamarra jacket
el champú shampoo
el chapoteadero kiddie pool
el chocolate chocolate
el/la chofer de autobús
  (m/f) bus driver
el cielo sky
cien hundred
la científica (f) scientist
el científico (m) scientist
el cilindro cylinder
cinco five
el cine movie theater
el cinturón belt
el círculo circle
el cirujano surgeon
el cisne swan
la ciudad town
la clase classroom
el clavo nail
el cobertizo shed
la cobija blanket
el cobrador (m) ticket collector
la cobradora (f) ticket collector
el coche car
el coche de policía police car
la cocina kitchen
cocinar cooking
la cocinera (f) chef
el cocinero (m) chef
el cocodrilo crocodile
el codo elbow
el cohete rocket

el cojín cushion
la col cabbage
la colcha comforter
la colina hill
el collar necklace
el collar de cuentas beads
los colores colors
el columpio swing
el comedero trough
el comedero de pájaros
  bird feeder
el comedor dining room
comer eating
el cometa comet
la cometa kite
la comida meal
la comida food
la cómoda dresser
la competencia competition
la computadora computer
la concha shell
el conductor (m) conductor
la conductora (f) conductor
el conejo rabbit
el continente continent
el control remoto
  remote control
el coral coral
el corazón heart
la corona crown
el corral yard
el corredor (m) jogger
la corredora (f) jogger
correr running
el cortacésped lawnmower
las cortinas curtains
corto/corta short
el costal sack
el cráneo skull
la cría del cisne baby swan
el cuadrado square
el cuadro painting
el cuadro picture
cuatro four
la cubeta bucket
el cubo cube
la cuchara spoon
el cuchillo knife
el cuello neck
la cuerda rope
la cuerda de saltar jump rope
el cuerpo body
el cuervo crow
el cumpleaños birthday
la cuna crib

la curita bandage
los dados dice
dar marometas doing
  somersaults
el dedo finger
el dedo del pie toe
el delantal apron
delante de in front of
el delfín dolphin
el/la dentista (m/f) dentist
el departamento apartment
los deportes sport
derecho/derecha right
el desayuno breakfast
desordenado/desordenada
  messy
el despertador alarm clock
detrás behind
las días days
dibujar drawing
el diccionario dictionary
diciembre December
diecinueve nineteen
dieciocho eighteen
dieciséis sixteen
diecisiete seventeen
los dientes teeth
diez ten
diferente different
el dinero money
el director (m) principal
la directora (f) principal
el disfraz de superhéroe
  superhero costume
doce twelve
el doctor (m) doctor
la doctora (f) doctor
dolor de cabeza headache
dolor de muelas toothache
dolor de panza tummy ache
domingo Sunday
el dominó dominoes
dorado gold
el dormitorio bedroom
dos two
el dragón dragon
la ducha shower
el durazno peach
el DVD DVD
él he
él him
el/la electricista
  (m/f) electrician
el elefante elephant
el elevador elevator

ella her
ella she
empujar pushing
en/sobre on
enero January
la enfermera (f) nurse
el enfermero (m) nurse
enfermo/enferma sick
enojado/enojada angry
la ensalada salad
el entrenador coach
el equipaje luggage
el equipo team
el equipo de deporte
  sports gear
escalar climbing
la escalera ladder
la escalera mecánica
  escalator
el escarabajo beetle
la escoba broom
escribir writing
la escuela school
la escultura sculpture
la esfera sphere
el esmalte de uñas nail polish
el espacio space
el espacio de lectura
  reading corner
la espalda back
el espantapájaros scarecrow
la espátula trowel
el espejo mirror
la esponja sponge
el esqueleto skeleton
esquiar skiing
los esquís skis
la estación de tren
  train station
las estaciones seasons
el estanque pond
estar parado standing
estar sentado sitting
el estetoscopio stethoscope
el/la estilista (m/f) hairdresser
la estrella de mar starfish
la estrella del pop singer
la estrella star
la estufa stove
la excavadora excavator
el extraterrestre alien
la fábrica factory
la falda skirt
la familia family
la farmacia pharmacy

el faro lighthouse
febrero February
feliz happy
feo/fea ugly
el ferry ferry
la fiesta party
la flauta recorder
la flor flower
el florero vase
el fondo del mar under the sea
las formas shapes
el fregadero sink
la fresa strawberry
frío/fría cold
la fruta fruit
el fuego fire
el/la futbolista
   (m/f) soccer player
el futbolito foosball table
las gafas de buceo goggles
la galaxia galaxy
la galería de arte art gallery
las galletas cookies
la gallina chicken
el ganso goose
el garage garage
la gasolinera gas station
gatear crawling
el gatito kitten
el gato cat
la gaviota seagull
las gemelas (f) twins
los gemelos (m) twins
el genio genie
el gigante giant
la gimnasia gymnastics
el globo balloon
el globo terráqueo globe
la glorieta roundabout
la goma de borrar eraser
el gorila gorilla
la gorra cap
la gráfica chart
grande big
el granero barn
el granizo hail
la granja farm
la granja farmhouse
la granjera (f) farmer
el granjero (m) farmer
gris gray
la grulla crane
los guantes gloves
el/la guardaparques
   (m/f) park ranger

el/la guarda del zoológico
   (m/f) zookeeper
la guitarra guitar
hablar talking
hacer volterete lateral
   doing a cartwheel
el hacha axe
el hada fairy
el hámster hamster
el helado ice cream
el helicóptero helicopter
el heno hay
la hermana sister
el hermano brother
hermoso/hermosa beautiful
el hexágono hexagon
el hielo ice
la hierba grass
la hija daughter
el hijo son
el hipopótamo hippopotamus
la hoja leaf
los hombros shoulders
el hospital hospital
el hotel hotel
hoy today
el huerto orchard
el huerto backyard
el huerto de verduras
   vegetable patch
el hueso bone
la huevera egg cup
los huevos eggs
igual same
el inodoro toilet
los instrumentos instruments
el invernadero greenhouse
el invierno winter
la inyección injection
izquierdo/izquierda left
jalar pulling
el jabón soap
el jamón ham
la jardinera (f) gardener
el jardinero (m) gardener
la jarra de agua pitcher
   of water
la jaula cage
la jirafa giraffe
joven young
el joyero jewelry box
el juego game
el juego de magia magic set
jueves Thursday
jugar playing

el jugo de fruta fruit juice
el jugo de naranja orange juice
los juguetes toys
julio July
la jungla jungle
junio June
el kiwi kiwi
el koala koala
el labio lip
el ladrillo brick
la lagartija lizard
el lago lake
la lámpara lamp
la lámpara de escritorio
   desk lamp
la lámpara mágica magic lamp
la lancha dinghy
la langosta lobster
los lápices de colores
   colored pencils
el lápiz pencil
la laptop laptop
largo/larga long
el lavabo sink
la lavadora washing machine
lavarse washing up
lavarse los dientes brushing
   your teeth
la leche milk
la lechuga lettuce
leer reading
la lengua tongue
los lentes glasses
los lentes de sol sunglasses
lento/lenta slow
el león lion
levantarse getting up
el librero bookshelf
el librero shelf
el libro book
el libro de cuentos storybook
el libro de texto textbook
ligero/ligera light
el limón lemon
la limonada lemonade
limpio/limpia clean
la línea de salida starting block
la llave key
lleno/llena full
la lluvia rain
el lobo wolf
el lodo mud
la lombriz worm
la luna moon
lunes Monday

la maceta flower pot
la madera wood
la madre mother
la madriguera burrow
la madriguera del ratón
   mouse hole
la maestra (f) teacher
el maestro (m) teacher
el mago magician
el maíz corn
la maleta suitcase
la maleta deportiva sports bag
malo/mala bad
mamá mom
mañana morning
las manchas stains
el mango mango
la manguera hose
la mano hand
la mantequilla butter
la manzana apple
el manzano apple tree
el mapa map
el mapache raccoon
el maquillaje make-up
la máquina de rayos X
   x-ray machine
el marcador scoreboard
el marco frame
la mariposa butterfly
martes Tuesday
el martillo hammer
marzo March
el matasuegras party blower
mayo May
la media luna crescent
las medias tights
la medicina medicine
la medusa jellyfish
la mejilla cheek
el mercado farmers' market
la merienda snack
la mermelada jam
la mesa table
los meses months
la mesita de noche
   bedside table
mí me
miércoles Wednesday
mil thousand
el minigolf miniature golf
la mochila backpack
mojado/mojada wet
el monedero purse
el mono monkey

la **montaña** mountain
morado/morada purple
la **morsa** walrus
la **mosca** fly
el **mosquito** mosquito
la **moto** all-terrain vehicle (ATV)
la **motocicleta** motorcycle
los **muebles** furniture
las **muletas** crutches
multicolor multicolored
la **muñeca** doll
el **muñeco de nieve** snowman
el **murciélago** bat
el **museo** museum
la **música** music
nadar swimming
la **naranja** orange (fruit)
naranja orange
la **nariz** nose
el **naufragio** shipwreck
la **neblina** fog
negro/negra black
la **nieve** snow
la **niña** girl
el **niño** boy
el **niño/la niña** child
noche night
el **nombre** name
noviembre November
la **nube** cloud
nueve nine
los **números** numbers
la **nutria** otter
la **obrera** (f) construction worker
el **obrero** (m) construction worker
el **océano** ocean
ocho eight
octubre October
la **oficina** office
la **oficina de correos** post office
los **oficios** jobs
los **ojos** eyes
la **ola** wave
la **olla** pot
once eleven
la **operación** operation
los **opuestos** opposites
la **órbita** orbit
ordenado/ordenada neat
la **oreja** ear
la **oruga** caterpillar
oscuro dark
el **osito de peluche** teddy bear

el **oso grizzly** grizzly bear
el **oso pardo** brown bear
el **oso polar** polar bear
el **otoño** fall
ovalado/ovalada oval
la **oveja** sheep
el **OVNI** UFO
el **padre** father
los **padres** parents
el **pájaro** bird
la **pala** shovel
las **palabras de acción** action words
la **paleta** palette
la **paleta de caramelo** lollipop
pálido/pálida pale
el **palo** stick
la **paloma** pigeon
palos para trepar jungle gym
el **pan** bread
la **panadera** (f) baker
la **panadería** bakery
el **panadero** (m) baker
el **panal** beehive
el **panda** panda
la **pantalla** lampshade
el **pantalón** pants
los **pantalones cortos** shorts
las **pantuflas** slippers
los **pañuelos desechables** tissues
la **panza** tummy
la **papa** potato
el **papá** dad
las **papas fritas** french fries
el **papel** paper
el **papel higiénico** toilet paper
la **parada del autobús** bus stop
el **paraguas** umbrella
pararse de cabeza doing a headstand
la **pared** wall
el **parque** park
el **parque infantil** playground
el **partido de fútbol** soccer game
el **pasillo** hallway
el **paso a nivel** railroad crossing
el **paso peatonal** crosswalk
la **pasta** pasta
la **pasta de dientes** toothpaste
el **pastel** cake

las **pastillas** pills
el **pasto** lawn
el **pastor** shepherd
los **patines** rollerblades
el **patito** duckling
el **pato** duck
el **pecho** chest
el **pegamento** glue
el **peine** comb
la **pelota** ball
la **pelota de playa** beach ball
los **peluches** stuffed animals
el **pepino** cucumber
pequeño/pequeña small
la **pera** pear
el **perico** parrot
el **perro** dog
el **perro pastor** sheepdog
pesado/pesada heavy
el **pescado** fish
pescar fishing
el **peso** weight
el **pez** fish (in water)
el **picnic** picnic
el **pie** foot
las **piedras** stones
la **pierna** leg
el **pijama** pajamas
pila para hacer compost compost pile
el/la **piloto** (m/f) pilot
la **piña** pineapple
el **pincel** paintbrush
el **ping pong** ping pong table
el **pingüino** penguin
pintar painting
las **pinturas** paints
la **pirámide** pyramid
el **pirata** pirate
el **piso** floor
la **pizarra blanca** whiteboard
la **pizza** pizza
los **planetas** planets
la **planta** plant
el **plátano** banana
plateado silver
el **platillo** saucer
los **platillos** cymbals
el **plato** plate
la **playa** beach
la **plomera** (f) plumber
el **plomero** (m) plumber
la **pluma** feather
la **pluma** shuttlecock
el/la **policía** (m/f) police officer

el **pollito** chick
el **pollo** chicken (to eat)
el **poncho** poncho
el **poni** pony
el **portero** goalie
el **posavasos** coaster
el **póster** poster
el **potro** foal
la **primavera** spring
primero/primera first
las **primas** (f) cousins
los **primos** (m) cousins
la **princesa** princess
el **príncipe** prince
el **puente** bridge
la **puerta** door
la **puerta** gate
el **puerto** port
el **puesto** stall
los **pulmones** lungs
el **pulpo** octopus
la **pulsera** bracelet
los **puntos** stitches
el **pupitre** desk
los **quequis** cupcakes
el **queso** cheese
quince fifteen
el **quiosco** gazebo
el **quirófano** operating room
la **radio** radio
la **radiografía** x-ray
la **rama** branch
la **rana** frog
rápido/rápida fast
la **raqueta** racket
el **rastrillo** rake
la **rata** rat
el **ratón** mouse
la **recolectora** combine harvester
el **rectángulo** rectangle
el **refresco** soda
el **refrigerador** fridge
el **refugio** shelter
la **regadera de plantas** watering can
el **regalo** present
la **regla** ruler
la **reina** queen
el **relámpago** lightning
el **reloj** clock
el **reloj** watch
el **remo** oar
el **remo** paddle
el **remolque** trailer
el **renacuajo** tadpole

el reno reindeer
el reposapiés footstool
la resbaladilla slide
el restaurante restaurant
el rey king
los rieles train tracks
el rinoceronte rhinoceros
el río stream
el río river
el robot robot
la roca rock
la rodilla knee
rojo/roja red
el rompecabezas jigsaw puzzle
la ropa clothes
rosa pink
ruidoso/ruidosa noisy
sábado Saturday
la sábana sheet
la sala de espera waiting room
la sala living room
las salchichas cocktail sausages
saltar jumping
el salto de altura high jump
el salto de longitud long jump
el salvavidas life preserver
el/la salvavidas (m/f) lifeguard
las sandalias sandals
el sándwich sandwich
sano/sana healthy
el satélite satellite
el sauna sauna
seco/seca dry
la secretaria secretary
seis six
el semáforo traffic light
la señal signal
la señal de tráfico traffic sign
señalar pointing
el sendero trail
septiembre September
la serpentina streamer
el serrucho saw
la servilleta napkin
el seto hedge
siete seven
el silbato whistle
silencioso/silenciosa quiet
la silla chair
la silla de ruedas wheelchair
la silla para bebé highchair
el sillón armchair
la sirena mermaid
la sobrina niece
el sobrino nephew
el sofá couch

el sol sun
el sombrero hat
el sombrero de fiesta party hat
la sombrilla beach umbrella
Sr. Mr.
Sra. Mrs.
el sube y baja seesaw
sucio/sucia dirty
el suéter sweater
el suéter abierto cardigan
el supermercado supermarket
el/la surfista (m/f) surfer
la suricata meerkat
la tabla de surf surfboard
la tablet tablet
el taburete stool
la tacita sippy cup
el tambor drum
el tapete bath mat
el tapete rug
la tarde afternoon
el/la taxista (m/f) taxi driver
la taza cup
el tazón bowl
el tazón wok
el té tea
el techo ceiling
el tejón badger
el teléfono telephone
la televisión television
el tenedor fork
el tenis tennis
el termómetro thermometer
la tetera teapot
la tía aunt
la tía abuela great-aunt
la tiara tiara
el tiburón shark
el tiempo weather
la tienda store
la tienda de campaña tent
la tienda de juguetes
 toy store
la tienda de libros book store
la tienda de mascotas
 pet store
la Tierra Earth
el tigre tiger
las tijeras scissors
la tina bath
el tinaco rain barrel
el tío uncle
el tío abuelo great-uncle
los títeres puppets
la toalla towel
el tobillo ankle

el tomate tomato
la tormenta storm
el tornado tornado
la tostada toast
el tractor tractor
el traje de baño swimsuit
el trampolín diving board
tranquila/ tranquilo calm
el transbordador espacial
 space shuttle
transparente transparent
el transporte transportation
el trapo de cocina dish towel
trece thirteen
el tren train
el trenecito de juguete
 toy train
tres three
el triángulo triangle
el triciclo tricycle
el trigo wheat
las trillizas (f) triplets
los trillizos (m) triplets
triste sad
la trompeta trumpet
el tronco log
tú you
el tubo tube
el túnel tunnel
turquesa turquoise
último/última last
las uñas nails
uno/una one
las uvas grapes
la vaca cow
las vacaciones vacation
vacío/vacía empty
la vajilla sucia dirty dishes
la varita mágica magic wand
el vaso glass
los vegetales vegetables
los vehículos vehicles
veinte twenty
la vela candle
el velero yacht
el venado deer
la venda bandage
el vendedor (m) sales associate
la vendedora (f) sales associate
la ventana window
ver la tele watching TV
el verano summer
verde green
el vestido dress
el vestido de fiesta
 party dress

el vestido de noche
 nightgown
el vestidor locker room
la veterinaria (f) vet
el veterinario (m) vet
el viaje travel
la víbora snake
viejo/vieja old
el viento wind
viernes Friday
el viñedo vineyard
violeta violet
el violín violin
los visitantes visitors
vívido/vívida vivid
el volquete dump truck
el xilófono xylophone
el yoga yoga
el yogurt yogurt
la zanahoria carrot
los zancos stilts
las zapatillas de ballet
 ballet slippers
los zapatos shoes
la zona de construcción
 construction site
el zoológico zoo
el zorro fox

English/inglés – Spanish/español

accident el accidente

action words las palabras de acción

aerobics los aeróbicos

afternoon la tarde

airplane el avión

airport el aeropuerto

alarm clock el despertador

alien el extraterrestre

all-terrain vehicle (ATV) la moto

alphabet el abecedario

ambulance la ambulancia

angry enojado/enojada

animals los animales

ankle el tobillo

apartment el departamento

apple la manzana

apple tree el manzano

April abril

apron el delantal

arm el brazo

armchair el sillón

art gallery la galería de arte

artist (m/f) el/la artista

asteroid el asteroide

astronaut el astronauta

athletics el atletismo

August agosto

aunt la tía

aviary el aviario

axe el hacha

baby el bebé

baby swan la cría del cisne

back la espalda

backpack la mochila

backyard el huerto

bad malo/mala

badger el tejón

badminton el bádminton

el bolso bag

baker (f) la panadera

baker (m) el panadero

bakery la panadería

ball la pelota

ballet slippers las zapatillas de ballet

balloon el globo

banana el plátano

bandage la venda

bandage la curita

bank el banco

barn el granero

basket la canasta

basketball el baloncesto

bat el murciélago

bath la tina

bath mat el tapete

bathroom el baño

beach la playa

beach ball la pelota de playa

beach umbrella la sombrilla

beads el collar de cuentas

beautiful hermoso/hermosa

beaver el castor

bed la cama

bedroom el dormitorio

bedside table la mesita de noche

beehive el panal

beetle el escarabajo

behind detrás

belt el cinturón

bench el banco

bib el babero

bicycle la bicicleta

big grande

binoculars los binoculares

bird el pájaro

bird feeder el comedero de pájaros

birthday el cumpleaños

black negro/negra

blanket la cobija

blocks los bloques

blue azul

boat el barco

body el cuerpo

bone el hueso

book el libro

book bag el bolso escolar

book store la tienda de libros

bookshelf el librero

boots las botas

bottle la botella

bowl el tazón

boy el niño

bracelet la pulsera

brain el cerebro

branch la rama

bread el pan

breakfast el desayuno

brick el ladrillo

bridge el puente

bright brillante

broom la escoba

brother el hermano

brown café

brown bear el oso pardo

brushing your teeth lavarse los dientes

bucket la cubeta

bulldozer el bulldozer

buoy la boya

burrow la madriguera

bus el autobús

bus driver (m/f) el/la chofer de autobús

bus stop la parada del autobús

bush el arbusto

butcher (f) la carnicera

butcher (m) el carnicero

butcher shop la carnicería

butter la mantequilla

butterfly la mariposa

cabbage la col

cabinet la alacena

cactus el cactus

café el café

cafeteria la cafetería

cage la jaula

cake el pastel

calf el becerro

calm tranquila/ tranquilo

campsite el campamento

candle la vela

canoe la canoa

cap la gorra

car el coche

cardigan el suéter abierto

carrot la zanahoria

carrying cargar

cash register la caja registradora

castle el castillo

cat el gato

caterpillar la oruga

ceiling el techo

celery el apio

cell phone el celular

cement mixer el camión de mezcla

cereal el cereal

chair la silla

chameleon el camaleón

chart la gráfica

cheek la mejilla

cheese el queso

chef (f) la cocinera

chef (m) el cocinero

cherry la cereza

chest el baúl

chest el pecho

chick el pollito

chicken la gallina

chicken (to eat) el pollo

child el niño/la niña

chin la barbilla

chocolate el chocolate

circle el círculo

classroom la clase

clean limpio/limpia

cleats las botas de fútbol

cliff el acantilado

climbing escalar

cloak la capa

clock el reloj

clothes la ropa

cloud la nube

coach el entrenador

coaster el posavasos

coat el abrigo

cocktail sausages las salchichas

coffee el café

cold frío/fría

colored pencils los lápices de colores

colors los colores

comb el peine

combine harvester la recolectora

comet el cometa

comforter la colcha

competition la competencia

compost pile pila para hacer compost

computer la computadora

conductor (m) el conductor

conductor (f) la conductora

construction site la zona de construcción

construction worker (f) la obrera

construction worker (m) el obrero

container ship el carguero

continent el continente

cookies las galletas

cooking cocinar

coral el coral

corn el maíz

cotton candy el algodón de azúcar

couch el sofá

countryside el campo

cousins (f) las primas

cousins (m) los primos

cow la vaca

crab el cangrejo

crane la grulla

crawling gatear

crescent la media luna

crib la cuna

crocodile el cocodrilo

English/inglés – Spanish/español

crosswalk el paso peatonal
crow el cuervo
crown la corona
crutches las muletas
cube el cubo
cucumber el pepino
cup la taza
cupcakes los quequis
curtains las cortinas
cushion el cojín
cylinder el cilindro
cymbals los platillos
dad el papá
dancer (m) el bailarín
dancer (f) la bailarina
dancing bailar
dark oscuro
daughter la hija
days las días
December diciembre
deckchair el camastro
deer el venado
dentist (m/f) el/la dentista
desk el pupitre
desk lamp la lámpara de
  escritorio
dice los dados
dictionary el diccionario
different diferente
dinghy la lancha
dining room el comedor
dirty sucio/sucia
dirty dishes la vajilla sucia
dish towel el trapo de cocina
diving board el trampolín
doctor (m) el doctor
doctor (f) la doctora
dog el perro
doing a cartwheel hacer
  volterete lateral
doing a headstand pararse
  de cabeza
doing somersaults dar
  marometas
doll la muñeca
doll house la casa de muñecas
dolphin el delfín
dominoes el dominó
door la puerta
dragon el dragón
drawing dibujar
dress el vestido
dresser la cómoda
drinking beber
drum el tambor
dry seco/seca

duck el pato
duckling el patito
dump truck el volquete
DVD el DVD
ear la oreja
Earth la Tierra
easel el caballete
eating comer
egg cup la huevera
eggplant la berenjena
eggs los huevos
eight ocho
eighteen dieciocho
elbow el codo
electrician (m/f) el/la electricista
elephant el elefante
elevator el elevador
eleven once
empty vacío/vacía
eraser la goma de borrar
escalator la escalera mecánica
excavator la excavadora
eyes los ojos
face la cara
factory la fábrica
fairy el hada
fall el otoño
family la familia
family tree el árbol genealógico
farm la granja
farmer (f) la granjera
farmer (m) el granjero
farmers' market el mercado
farmhouse la granja
fast rápido/rápida
father el padre
feather la pluma
February febrero
fence la cerca
ferry el ferry
field el campo
fifteen quince
finger el dedo
fire el fuego
fire engine el camión de bomberos
firefighter (f) la bombera
firefighter (m) el bombero
first primero/primera
fish el pescado
fish (in water) el pez
fishing pescar
fishing boat el barco de pesca
five cinco
flag la bandera
flight attendant (f) la aeromoza
flight attendant (m) el aeromozo

floor el piso
flower la flor
flower pot la maceta
fly la mosca
foal el potro
fog la neblina
food la comida
foosball table el futbolito
foot el pie
forest el bosque
fork el tenedor
footstool el reposapiés
four cuatro
fourteen catorce
fox el zorro
frame el marco
french fries las papas fritas
Friday viernes
fridge el refrigerador
friend (f) la amiga
friend (m) el amigo
friends (f) las amigas
friends (m) los amigos
frog la rana
fruit la fruta
fruit juice el jugo de fruta
full lleno/llena
furniture los muebles
galaxy la galaxia
game el juego
garage el garage
gardener (f) la jardinera
gardener (m) el jardinero
gas station la gasolinera
gate la puerta
gazebo el quiosco
genie el genio
getting up levantarse
giant el gigante
giraffe la jirafa
girl la niña
glass el vaso
glasses los lentes
globe el globo terráqueo
gloves los guantes
glue el pegamento
goalie el portero
goat la cabra
goggles las gafas de buceo
going to sleep acostarse
gold dorado
good bueno/buena
goose el ganso
gorilla el gorila
grandfather el abuelo
grandmother la abuela

grandparents los abuelos
grapes las uvas
grass la hierba
gray gris
great-aunt la tía abuela
great-grandparents
  los bisabuelos
great-uncle el tío abuelo
green verde
greenhouse el invernadero
grizzly bear el oso grizzly
guitar la guitarra
gymnastics la gimnasia
hail el granizo
hair el cabello
hairbrush el cepillo del cabello
hairdresser (m/f) el/la estilista
hallway el pasillo
ham el jamón
hammer el martillo
hamster el hámster
hand la mano
happy feliz
hat el sombrero
hay el heno
he él
head la cabeza
headache dolor de cabeza
headphones los audífonos
healthy sano/sana
heart el corazón
heavy pesado/pesada
hedge el seto
height la altura
helicopter el helicóptero
her ella
hexagon el hexágono
high jump el salto de altura
highchair la silla para bebé
hill la colina
him él
hippopotamus el hipopótamo
home la casa
horse el caballo
hose la manguera
hospital el hospital
hot caliente
hotel el hotel
house la casa
hug abrazo
hugging abrazar
hundred cien
ice el hielo
ice cream el helado
in front of delante de
injection la inyección

instruments los instrumentos
jacket la chamarra
jam la mermelada
January enero
jellyfish la medusa
jewelry box el joyero
jigsaw puzzle el rompecabezas
jobs los oficios
jogger (m) el corredor
jogger (f) la corredora
July julio
jump rope la cuerda de saltar
jumping saltar
June junio
jungle la jungla
jungle gym palos para trepar
kangaroo el canguro
key la llave
kid (baby goat) el cabrito
kiddie pool el chapoteadero
king el rey
kiss beso
kissing besar
kitchen la cocina
kite la cometa
kitten el gatito
kiwi el kiwi
knee la rodilla
knife el cuchillo
knight el caballero
koala el koala
ladder la escalera
lake el lago
lamb el borrego
lamp la lámpara
lampshade la pantalla
laptop la laptop
last último/última
lawn el pasto
lawnmower el cortacésped
lawyer (f) la abogada
lawyer (m) el abogado
leaf la hoja
left izquierdo/izquierda
leg la pierna
lemonade la limonada
lemon el limón
letter la carta
lettuce la lechuga
library la biblioteca
life jacket el chaleco salvavidas
lifeguard (m/f) el/la salvavidas
life preserver el salvavidas
light ligero/ligera
lighthouse el faro
lightning el relámpago

lion el león
lip el labio
living room la sala
lizard la lagartija
lobster la langosta
locker room el vestidor
log el tronco
lollipop la paleta de caramelo
long largo/larga
long jump el salto de longitud
luggage el equipaje
lungs los pulmones
magic lamp la lámpara mágica
magic set el juego de magia
magic wand la varita mágica
magician el mago
mail carrier el cartero
mailbag la bolsa del cartero
mailbox el buzón
make-up el maquillaje
mango el mango
map el mapa
March marzo
May mayo
me mí
meal la comida
medicine la medicina
meerkat la suricata
mermaid la sirena
messy desordenado/
  desordenada
milk la leche
miniature golf el minigolf
mirror el espejo
model airplane el avión armable
mom mamá
Monday lunes
money el dinero
monkey el mono
months los meses
moon la luna
morning mañana
mosquito el mosquito
mother la madre
motorcycle la motocicleta
mountain la montaña
mountain bike la bicicleta
  de montaña
mouse el ratón
mouse hole la madriguera
  del ratón
mouth la boca
movie theater el cine
Mr. Sr.
Mrs. Sra.
mud el lodo

multicolored multicolor
museum el museo
music la música
nail el clavo
nail polish el esmalte de uñas
nails las uñas
name el nombre
napkin la servilleta
neat ordenado/ordenada
neck el cuello
necklace el collar
nephew el sobrino
niece la sobrina
night noche
nightgown el vestido de noche
nine nueve
nineteen diecinueve
noisy ruidoso/ruidosa
nose la nariz
November noviembre
numbers los números
nurse (f) la enfermera
nurse (m) el enfermero
oar el remo
ocean el océano
October octubre
octopus el pulpo
office la oficina
old viejo/vieja
on en/sobre
one uno/una
onion la cebolla
operating room el quirófano
operation la operación
opposites los opuestos
orange naranja
orange (fruit) la naranja
orange juice el jugo de naranja
orbit la órbita
orchard el huerto
otter la nutria
oval ovalado/ovalada
owl el búho
paddle el remo
pager el buscapersonas
paintbrush el pincel
painting pintar
painting el cuadro
paints las pinturas
pajamas el pijama
pale pálido/pálida
palette la paleta
panda el panda
pants el pantalón
paper el papel
parents los padres

park el parque
park ranger
  (m/f) el/la guardaparques
parrot el perico
party la fiesta
party blower el matasuegras
party dress el vestido
  de fiesta
party hat el sombrero
  de fiesta
pasta la pasta
path el camino
peach el durazno
pear la pera
pen el bolígrafo
pencil el lápiz
penguin el pingüino
pet store la tienda de mascotas
pharmacy la farmacia
picnic el picnic
picture el cuadro
pig el cerdo
pigeon la paloma
piglet el cerdito
pillow la almohada
pills las pastillas
pilot (m/f) el/la piloto
pineapple la piña
ping pong table el ping pong
pink rosa
pirate el pirata
pitcher of water la jarra
  de agua
pizza la pizza
planets los planetas
plant la planta
plate el plato
platform el andén
playground el parque infantil
playing jugar
plumber (f) la plomera
plumber (m) el plomero
pocket el bolsillo
pointing señalar
polar bear el oso polar
police car el coche de policía
police officer (m/f) el/la policía
poncho el poncho
pond el estanque
pony el poni
port el puerto
post office la oficina de correos
poster el póster
pot la olla
potato la papa
present el regalo

prince el príncipe
princess la princesa
principal (f) la directora
principal (m) el director
public restroom el baño público
pulling jalar
puppets los títeres
puppy el cachorro
purple morado/morada
purse el monedero
purse la bolsa
pushing empujar
pyramid la pirámide
queen la reina
quiet silencioso/silenciosa
rabbit el conejo
race la carrera
raccoon el mapache
racket la raqueta
radio la radio
railroad crossing el paso a nivel
rain la lluvia
rain barrel el tinaco
rain boots las botas
  de agua
rainbow el arco iris
rake el rastrillo
rat la rata
reading leer
reading corner el espacio
  de lectura
rec center el centro deportivo
recorder la flauta
rectangle el rectángulo
red rojo/roja
referee el árbitro
reindeer el reno
remote control el control
  remoto
restaurant el restaurante
rhinoceros el rinoceronte
rice el arroz
riding a bike andar
  en bicicleta
right derecho/derecha
ring el anillo
river el río
robot el robot
rock la roca
rocket el cohete
rocking horse el caballo
  mecedor
rollerblades los patines
rope la cuerda
roundabout la glorieta
row boat el bote de remo

rug el tapete
ruler la regla
running correr
sack el costal
sad triste
salad la ensalada
sales associate
  (m) el vendedor
sales associate
  (f) la vendedora
same igual
sand la arena
sandals las sandalias
sandbox el arenero
sandcastle el castillo
  de arena
sandwich el sándwich
sanitation worker
  (f) la basurera
sanitation worker
  (m) el basurero
satellite el satélite
Saturday sábado
saucer el platillo
sauna el sauna
saw el serrucho
scaffolding el andamio
scarecrow
  el espantapájaros
scarf la bufanda
school la escuela
scientist (f) la científica
scientist (m) el científico
scissors las tijeras
scoreboard el marcador
scuba diver el buceador
sculpture la escultura
seagull la gaviota
seasons las estaciones
seat el asiento
seaweed el alga marina
secretary la secretaria
seesaw el sube y baja
semi/tractor trailer el camión
September septiembre
seven siete
seventeen diecisiete
shampoo el champú
shapes las formas
shark el tiburón
she ella
shed el cobertizo
sheep la oveja
sheepdog el perro pastor
sheet la sábana
shelf el librero

shell la concha
shelter el refugio
shepherd el pastor
ship el barco
shipwreck el naufragio
shirt la camisa
shoes los zapatos
shopping bag la bolsa
  de compras
shopping cart el carrito
short corto/corta
shorts los pantalones cortos
shoulders los hombros
shovel la pala
shower la ducha
shuttlecock la pluma
sick enfermo/enferma
sideboard/buffet el aparador
sidewalk la acera
signal la señal
signpost el cartel
silver plateado
singer la estrella del pop
singing cantar
sink el lavabo
sink el fregadero
sippy cup la tacita
sister la hermana
sitting estar sentado
six seis
sixteen dieciséis
skeleton el esqueleto
skiing esquiar
skirt la falda
skis los esquís
skull el cráneo
sky el cielo
slide la resbaladilla
sling el cabestrillo
slippers las pantuflas
slow lento/lenta
small pequeño/pequeña
snack la merienda
snail el caracol
snake la víbora
snow la nieve
snowman el muñeco de nieve
soap el jabón
soccer ball el balón de fútbol
soccer game el partido
  de fútbol
soccer player
  (m/f) el/la futbolista
socks los calcetines
soda el refresco
son el hijo

space el espacio
space shuttle
  el transbordador espacial
speakers las bocinas
sphere la esfera
spider la araña
sponge la esponja
spoon la cuchara
sport los deportes
sports bag la maleta deportiva
sports gear el equipo
  de deporte
spring la primavera
square el cuadrado
squirrel la ardilla
stains las manchas
stall el puesto
standing estar parado
star la estrella
starfish la estrella de mar
starting block la línea de salida
stethoscope el estetoscopio
stick el palo
stilts los zancos
stitches los puntos
stones las piedras
stool el taburete
store la tienda
storm la tormenta
storybook el libro de cuentos
stove la estufa
strawberry la fresa
stream el río
streamer la serpentina
street/road la calle
stroller la carriola
student (f) la alumna
student (m) el alumno
stuffed animals los peluches
suitcase la maleta
summer el verano
sun el sol
Sunday domingo
sunglasses los lentes de sol
sunscreen el bloqueador
superhero costume el disfraz
  de superhéroe
supermarket el supermercado
surfboard la tabla de surf
surfer (m/f) el/la surfista
surgeon el cirujano
swan el cisne
sweater el suéter
swimming nadar
swimming pool la alberca
swimsuit el traje de baño

English/inglés – Spanish/español

swing el columpio
table la mesa
tablet la tablet
tadpole el renacuajo
talking hablar
taxi driver (m/f) el/la taxista
tea el té
teacher (f) la maestra
teacher (m) el maestro
team el equipo
teapot la tetera
teddy bear el osito de peluche
teeth los dientes
telephone el teléfono
television la televisión
ten diez
tennis el tenis
tennis court la cancha de tenis
tent la tienda de campaña
textbook el libro de texto
thermometer el termómetro
thirteen trece
thousand mil
three tres
Thursday jueves
tiara la tiara
ticket el billete
ticket collector (f) la cobradora
ticket collector (m) el cobrador
tiger el tigre
tights las medias
tissues los pañuelos desechables
toast la tostada
today hoy
toe el dedo del pie
toilet el inodoro
toilet paper el papel higiénico
tomato el tomate
tongue la lengua
toolbox la caja de herramientas
toothache dolor de muelas

toothbrush el cepillo de dientes
toothpaste la pasta de dientes
tornado el tornado
towel la toalla
town la ciudad
toy store la tienda de juguetes
toy train el trenecito de juguete
toys los juguetes
tractor el tractor
traffic light el semáforo
traffic sign la señal de tráfico
trail el sendero
trailer el remolque
train el tren
train station la estación de tren
train tracks los rieles
transparent transparente
transportation el transporte
trash can el bote de basura
travel el viaje
tree el árbol
treehouse la casita del árbol
triangle el triángulo
tricycle el triciclo
triplets (f) las trillizas
triplets (m) los trillizos
trough el comedero
trowel la espátula
truck driver (f) la camionera
truck driver (m) el camionero
trumpet la trompeta
T-shirt la camiseta
tube el tubo
Tuesday martes
tummy la panza
tummy ache dolor de panza
tunnel el túnel

turquoise turquesa
twelve doce
twenty veinte
twins (f) las gemelas
twins (m) los gemelos
two dos
UFO el OVNI
ugly feo/fea
umbrella el paraguas
uncle el tío
under bajo
under the sea el fondo del mar
underwear los calzones
vacation las vacaciones
vacuum cleaner la aspiradora
van la camioneta
vase el florero
vegetable patch el huerto de verduras
vegetables los vegetales
vehicles los vehículos
vest el chaleco
vet (f) la veterinaria
vet (m) el veterinario
vineyard el viñedo
violet violeta
violin el violín
visitors los visitantes
vivid vívido/vívida
waiting room la sala de espera
walking andar
walking boots las botas
walking stick el bastón
wall la pared
walrus la morsa
wardrobe el armario
washing machine la lavadora
washing up lavarse
watch el reloj
watching TV ver la tele
water el agua
waterfall la cascada

watering can la regadera de plantas
wave la ola
weather el tiempo
Wednesday miércoles
weight el peso
wet mojado/mojada
whale la ballena
wheat el trigo
wheelbarrow la carretilla
wheelchair la silla de ruedas
whistle el silbato
white blanco/blanca
whiteboard la pizarra blanca
wind el viento
window la ventana
winter el invierno
witch la bruja
wok el tazón
wolf el lobo
wood la madera
worm la lombriz
writing escribir
x-ray la radiografía
x-ray machine la máquina de rayos X
xylophone el xilófono
yacht el velero
yard el corral
year el año
yellow amarillo
yesterday ayer
yoga el yoga
yogurt el yogurt
you tú
young joven
zebra la cebra
zoo el zoológico
zookeeper (m/f) el/la guarda del zoológico
zucchini el calabacín

My First 1000 Spanish Words: A Search-and-Find Book, New Edition © b small publishing ltd.

This edition © 2022 Happy Fox Books, an imprint of
Fox Chapel Publishing Company, Inc.,
903 Square Street, Mount Joy, PA 17552.
First published in 2014 by b small publishing ltd.

Illustrations: Stu McLellan
Design: Louise Millar
Editorial: Sam Hutchinson & Susan Martineau
Spanish advisers: Diego Blasco Vázquez & Trine Rasmussen
Spanish advisor, Happy Fox edition: Rosi Perea

Library of Congress Control Number: 2022936150

ISBN 978-1-64124-194-6

We are always looking for talented authors. To submit an idea, please send a brief inquiry to
acquisitions@foxchapelpublishing.com.

Printed in China
First printing